The Cabin
and
the River

Love stories from Up North

authorHOUSE®

AuthorHouse™
1663 Liberty Drive
Bloomington, IN 47403
www.authorhouse.com
Phone: 1-800-839-8640

First published by AuthorHouse 4/7/2011

ISBN: 978-1-4567-3746-7 (e)
ISNB: 978-1-4567-3747-4 (sc)

Library of Congress Control Number: 2011901879

Printed in the United States of America

*Any people depicted in stock imagery provided by Thinkstock are models,
and such images are being used for illustrative purposes only.
Certain stock imagery* © *Thinkstock.*

This book is printed on acid-free paper.

Dedicated with loving memory
to
Shirley Helen Causgrove

August 28, 1924 - December 4, 2005

PART ONE

BEFORE THE CABIN

My grandparents built a small rustic hunting cabin deep in the Huron Forest in northern Michigan, near the Au Sable River, back in the 1940s. No one has used it for hunting for decades; it's now used as a welcome place to which we can escape when we need some peace and relaxation. Our families, friends, and extended families have been taking vacations up there for over sixty years; to us, having a place up north for that long makes us feel like we somehow have an inherent seniority.

In reality we, as descendants of European settlers, have only been able to call Michigan our home for two hundred years or so. That land up north that we hike through year after year has been traversed, hunted on and cultivated long before the first settlers staked their claims.

When I am up at our cabin, I do often wonder about the people who lived there when my relatives were doggedly making a life for themselves in Germany and Prussia. Who else has walked through these woods? My family has a favorite spot to go to along the river, where the forest clears and we can walk in the sand down to the water. Long before we began taking our vacations there, I can guess that many people before us have loved and claimed this spot too and there will be countless visitors after us who will feel the same way about it. We often go there to swim, have campfires, river gaze, watch for bald eagles, and throw sticks for our dogs as far out into the Au Sable as we can. Sitting on the quiet river bank at the forest's edge, it is easy to feel somehow connected with the past; we become curious about the history of this peaceful place.

What about the people who were here first? Sitting on the top of a steep sandy bluff with the quiet Au Sable slowly flowing by below, it is hard to resist wondering about the people who had a claim to the forest before us.

****

Centuries before tourists began driving in droves to northern Michigan to escape from the stress of the cities and regain personal peace, there were a quiet people who lived there; they were more a part of the land than they were inhabitants of the land. They would not have understood using the rivers, lakes, and forests as simply places to relax; they needed those things to survive.

These people were the Ojibwe, Americanized to Chippewa; the eldest among them still use an even older word, Anishinabe, which means "original people". Together with the Ottawa and the Potawatomi, these three groups, the Council of Three Fires, formed a powerful, proud alliance of Native American tribes that stretched across the north-central United States and Southern Canada.

The Ojibwe lived in year-round settlements in what is now the Huron Forest and state park. They were a peaceful people, rightfully calling the woods and rivers of Michigan their own. When called upon to protect those beautiful forests however, they were known to answer fiercely and decisively.

For time unknown, the Ojibwe women gathered fruit and nuts from the forests, harvested rice, and tapped maple sugar from the abundant trees in spring. They wore beautiful, ankle-length deerskin robes that they beaded with stones and shells. Ojibwe men hunted deer and elk in the forests, and pulled boatloads of fish from the rivers. They protected their families when they had to. They loved the summers and somehow survived the bitter, harsh northern winters. The Ojibwe people had medicine men and women, and kept their history alive with music and story-telling.

When the French traders came to Michigan, the Ojibwe traded peacefully with them, beaver pelts for guns. And when the European settlers came, these brave people did their best too, to protect what had been theirs; in the end, they were no match for superior fire power, disease, trickery, and sheer numbers.

Large numbers of Ojibwe still live on reservations in Michigan, Minnesota, Wisconsin, and southern Canada. They have modernized of course, and most no longer hunt or fish to feed their families. These people who refused to die survived the decimation of their tribes, the often unjust progress of settlement. Their past has survived through their unique art of music and storytelling; they pass on their history from mother to child, and keep the soul of the Anishinabe alive.

CHAPTER ONE

Rolling Pebble, Little Bird, and the River
Early 1700s

It was a cool autumn morning on the big river of sand, during the time of the Falling Leaves Moon.

Rolling Pebble woke up early that morning; she couldn't sleep. Expectation and eagerness woke her up, refusing to let her lie on her bed any longer. Noiselessly she stepped outside the round, birch wigwam she shared with her family and looking up, squinted her eyes at the early sun. She stood straight, letting the crisp morning air blow across her dark face and toss her long brown hair around her.

This young Ojibwe woman had been counting the days till this morning for weeks; tonight there was going to be a feast in their camp, to honor and to ceremoniously name a baby boy born to her best friend Little Bird. Newborns were especially celebrated and honored among the Ojibwe, their arrivals marked with days of musical celebrations, and ending with a lively feast and dancing under the hazy sky and bright moon.

Rolling Pebble and Little Bird had been inseparable since birth; they were born 16 years earlier, just a few months apart. Theirs was a deep friendship and they shared everything, laughter and tears, stories and secrets. In her young heart, Rolling Pebble hoped to soon be married to a handsome, strong Ojibwe too, like her friend. She knew her time would come; her mother had taught her the patience of her people.

It was the responsibility of the clan elders to choose a name for the baby boy; the younger women in the tribe had to gather baskets of fruits, berries, and nuts for the feast. The somber, tradition-filled naming ceremony would be nicely rounded off by the meal of venison, fish, fruits, nuts, sunflower soup, wild rice, and sweet maple syrup treats.

Rolling Pebble shook free from her lazy daydreaming; it was long past time to be on the move. Most of the women in the tribe hunted for berries in groups; she liked to go to this certain spot alone. She brushed her long hair out of her face, picked up her birch basket and turned her feet in the direction of the river.

She knew exactly where to go that morning, knew that the best place to find plump fruit, ripe berries, and trees full of nuts was near the gentle banks of the quiet sandy river.

The walk to the river was a short one; her people lived very near the big river, a never-ending source of fish, beaver, and venison. The elders had also chosen to be near the wide, winding river because of the many birch trees; her people were already known far and wide for their ingenuity in creating birch bark baskets and especially canoes. Rolling Pebble and the other women in her clan spent countless hours pulling off precious strips of birch to cover their wigwams, which protected their families from the often harsh elements of upper Lower Michigan.

Today though, she didn't have to think about her chores; she only wanted to think about the dinner, the singing, the fairy tales and the dancing around the campfires with friends and family.

The sun was rising and she quickened her pace.

Rolling Pebble as usual had gotten an early start that morning. This was her favorite time of the day; the woods around her were beginning to come alive. Tiny chickadees and sparrows flitted in the treetops, singing in the morning sun. The gentle breeze, with an early hint of fall, blew across her face as she crunched over the dried, scrubby branches which poked at her as she pushed deeper into the forest.

Minutes passed, and she could smell the sand grass and other fragrant river smells now; she was getting closer. These woods near the river bank were very dense, the white pine, fir, maple, and birch trees all crowding each other for space. But to Rolling Pebble, cutting through the woods with ease was second nature; this was her land, her forest, and had been the land of her people forever before her. This big sandy river and the forest it cut through had unselfishly provided her people food, water, and shelter for as long as even her great grandfather could remember. Songs had been sung about this river over and over again around their fires at night.

The Ojibwe were a thankful nation, and Rolling Pebble owed thanks to the Great Spirit for many things. Today she gave thanks for the river, the deer, the beaver, the turkey, and new baby boys. She continued to push through the quiet forest, her moccasins crunching towards the river bank. The birch trees were thick here; it didn't matter that the beaver had been here too, gnawing down many of the trees and dragging them off to their river dens. The maples had begun their vivid color change only a week before; brilliant splashes of deep red, orange, and yellow caught her eye as she glanced up at the bright blue sky.

Gradually, the soil beneath her feet began to change from dirt to sand. Rolling Pebble began looking to her left, knowing she would soon catch glimpses of the river between the trees. Now she could even see the far banks across the river, crowded with dark green pine; the white birch and showy maple had to fight for room. She loved the quiet she felt in the woods near the river when she was by herself, which is why she chose to come alone. She stopped for a moment to enjoy the silence of the forest before walking on.

As Rolling Pebble got closer to the river bank, she began to methodically pick the plump elderberries and grapes which still clung heavy to the vines. Blueberries, blackberries, gooseberries or raspberries would be a real find, and she kept her brown eyes alert for those treasures. She thought again about the ceremony that night, her mouth watering at the thought of the smoked venison and fish that her mother and other senior women of the village were already preparing.

Most of the food for the feast tonight had been gathered in the past months. Wild rice was harvested in the month before this, during the Wild Rice Moon. The maple syrup had been tapped and heated and then stored, back in the months when the first warmth returned to the forest after the snow; the best time to tap the maple trees for the sweet syrup was when it was cold at night and warm during the day. The best cuts of deer and fish had been saved and put aside for the ceremony tonight, and the women had been gathering extra bark and fashioning it into a new canoe as a gift to the groom and his bride, to be given to them tonight after the naming of their baby boy.

She continued through the forest, picking as she went. She caught a glimpse of the deep sandy river as the morning sun glinted on a calm inlet; tiny waves sparkled in the morning sun. A shiny fish jumped in the middle of the river and then another; this was the best spot for the men in her camp to come and fish.

Rolling Pebble was good at collecting berries, and by now her birch basket was more than half full. Early morning had had a chill to it but now that the sun was in the middle of the sky she felt warm and thirsty; she pushed her way down to the river for a drink. She headed for an opening in the forest which she knew lead to a sandy path to the water. Here she could kneel down and get a drink from this gentle, giant river that was so clear and beautiful, she could see right to the bottom. The sun warmed her as she came out into the open; the sand parted under her feet as she slowly made her way to the clear cold water. She knelt down and drank her fill.

Glancing at the sky, she knew she had to hurry a little; she still needed to fill her basket and get back to the village to help the other women make the final preparations for the feast. She was needed too to help watch the younger children and decorate the camp for the ceremony. Rolling Pebble picked up her basket and slinging it on her hip, headed back into the woods.

It was afternoon when Rolling Pebble's basket was nearly too heavy with berries for her to carry, and she turned to head back to her camp. She chose her favorite path that wandered along the sandy bluff of the river. Even though she saw it every day, she was still awed by the calm, deep beauty of the river every time she looked at it. She glanced up as a flock of geese honked above her head, beating their powerful wings in their traditional "V" back to the north where their winter home was. She watched the beaver swimming around near the shore, busily working to strengthen their underwater homes for the upcoming months of ice, wind, and cold.

Rolling Pebble knew that her mother would need her back at the camp soon; she had to pull herself away and get back. She reached the spot where she must finally turn away from the river, and headed back into the deep woods towards home.

"Aaniin", Rolling Pebble greeted her mother back at camp. She set down her basket and her little sister and brother ran up to her, dropping their cornhusk dolls to hug her knees. She picked up her little sister and kissed her cheek, and stopped to watch the older kids finish a game of lacrosse. The venison was smoking, people were singing, and the camp looked festive; the evening would be a good one.

Only one thing had troubled Rolling Pebble that day. The Frenchmen that her father and brothers traded with had begun to speak of many white men coming. The traders said the men coming wanted their land; she didn't understand that. She heard they had guns and horses too. She pushed those thoughts out of her mind; surely the elders and the warriors could protect them from the new invaders. She could not imagine the river and the forest ever belonging to anyone else. Surely this river and the forests would be part of her people forever.

****

"Articles of a treaty made and concluded at Detroit, in the state of Michigan, on the fourteenth day of January, in the year of our Lord eighteen hundred and thirty-seven, between the United States of America by their commissioner, Henry R. Schoolcraft, and the Saganaw tribe of the Chippewa (Ojibwe) nation, by their chiefs and delegates, assembled in council.

Article 1st: The said tribe cede to the United States the following tracts of land, lying within the boundaries of Michigan; namely; One tract of eight thousand acres, on the river Au Sable...

Article 2d: ...the said Indians shall have the right of living upon the tracts at the river Augrais, and Mushowusk or Rifle rivers, on the west side of Saganaw bay, for the term of five years, during which no white man shall be allowed to settle on said tracts...

Article 3rd: The United States agree to pay to the said Indians, in consideration of the lands above ceded, the net proceeds of the sales thereof, after deducting the expense of survey and sale...the lands shall be surveyed in the usual manner, and offered for sale, as other public lands...

Article 6th: The said tribe agrees to remove from the State of Michigan, as soon as a proper location can be obtained...if an arrangement for their future and permanent residence can be made in that quarter (west of the most westernly point of Lake Superior), which shall be satisfactory to them, and to the Government, they shall be permitted to form a reunion, with such tribes, and remove thereto. If such arrangement cannot be effeced, the United States will afford its influence in obtaining a location for them at such place, west of the Mississippi, and southwest of the Missouri, as the legislation of Congress may indicate. The agency of the exploration,

9

purchase, and removal will be performed by the United States, but the expenses attending the same shall be chargeable to said Indians..."

CHAPTER TWO

The Au Sable River is known for many things. It is known for its beauty, for its famous yearly canoe race, for the bald eagles that nest along its banks. Looking back hundreds of years, fishermen knew it for the grayling; Native Americans pulled lake sturgeon from it, and modern fishermen cast their rods for the brown trout.

Running west to east 140 miles through the northern lower peninsula of Michigan, the Au Sable is home to countless summer cabins with private boat docks, and also permanent residents who have settled there after they found it just too hard to go back to the suburbs and cities. There are endless miles of hiking trails along the river; the views on top of the dunes are legendary. Six hydro-electric dams along the river provide power to thousands of citizens in northern Michigan.

This storied river has etched still another place in Michigan history: the Lumber Era. In the 1860's, the booming U.S. infrastructure demanded finished white pine. Developers needed the lumber for schools and homes; commercial steam ships that chugged up and down the Great Lakes by the hundreds needed logs to power their vessels. People turned to the forests and the rivers of Northern Michigan, which offered lumber in its raw form for miles and miles, as far as the eye could see. The other necessary ingredient was the manpower to extract and produce the final finished product, and a force of young, strong men answered the call.

Along the silent river in the dead of winter, hardy lumbermen felled the giant evergreens by the thousands. Draft horses dragged them to the sloping banks, where they were then rolled onto the waiting frozen river; with the spring thaw, they'd begin their journey to the Lake Huron sawmills and beyond.

Thanks in large part to the Au Sable, Michigan was the greatest producer of lumber from 1869 to 1900. The majority of homes and schools in the Midwest were built with Michigan white pine lumber. Nearly all European backgrounds were represented in the lumber camps of the Michigan forests, as men in search of steady work and pay jumped ships or railcars heading north. Upon arrival, they were handed steel axes and saws, and sent off into the forests to start work at the hardest job they would ever undertake.

George, Eddie, and the River
1800s

In the late 1800's, Detroit was a city struggling to recover from the Civil War. George Kapalski was born during the war to hard-working parents on a working-classs street.   His childhood friend Eddie O'Riordan was also born during the war, to tenacious Irish immigrants on a neighboring street. The boys went to the same schools starting in the first grade, and were best friends on up through high school.

The city of Detroit existed and prospered because of Lake Erie trading routes. By the 1820's, it had become a city of flour mills, refined flour being the major export. Factories that produced flour mill parts, businesses that fixed factory parts, and shipyards for sending off the finished product rounded out the economy. For the times, Detroit was a bustling, crowded and lively city. The streets were noisy and busy, and the factories created an urban skyline that blocked the natural one. But there was more to Michigan than just the city of Detroit; hundreds of miles to the north were vast expanses of seemingly endless forests, cool in the summer and quiet and peaceful in the winter.

George and Eddie graduated from high school in 1883. It was their rite of passage, their time to prove themselves and leave the classrooms behind. These two young men had watched their parents struggle to make ends meet year after year; they felt that in Detroit their choices and chances in life were few. They could work in the salt mines; they could work in the flour mills; they could work in the steel plants like Eddie's brothers; they could work in the growing shipping industry. None of these things appealed to them though; George and Eddie both wanted more, wanted to escape the city grind and break the mold. They felt there had to be something better. That fall, they put their heads together and started to search.

Weeks and months passed since graduation, and the two friends were growing frustrated trying to find meaningful work. For the short-term, they filled the days working odd jobs for the newspapers and taking on other miscellaneous errands.

Of the two, Eddie tended to be impulsive, and George was the more rational. Eddie had had several ideas for where they could find work and a future, which George quickly discounted as being mere wild schemes with no substance. George wasn't sure what he was looking for, but he knew he'd know it when he found it.

Eddie's latest idea was for the two of them to catch a ship up to the Soo

Locks in the upper peninsula of Michigan. He claimed men were needed to build the Locks and the pay was decent; he tried to convince his friend they should make the trip north. George wasn't sold on the Locks idea, but there was an allure and mystery about the great forests up north that appealed to him. Of course he didn't admit that to his friend right away; George needed to think about it for a bit.

However, Eddie had certainly planted a seed in his friend's mind. George woke early the next morning and dressed, barely finishing the breakfast his mother had ready for him on their old wooden table in the kitchen. He hurried in the morning summer sun along the already bustling Detroit market streets to a produce stand run by his longtime friend Frankie. He had met Frank through Eddie, and Frankie felt like an older brother to George. He trusted Frank; Frank got around and always seemed to know things. George never knew how Frank got his information or how he knew so much; after all, he was only a fruit seller.

George waited impatiently while Frank bagged up apples and grapes for an elderly woman, and leaned towards him with nervous, secretive excitement.

"Hey Frankie!" Frank turned around with a smile, recognizing the voice of his friend.

The first thing he asked George was about his search for work.

"Got a job yet??"

George said not yet, but he and Eddie were getting close. He wanted to ask Frank about the work at the Soo; what would Frank think about that? Frank rubbed his chin and thought for a minute. In his opinion, Frank told George the work at the Soo might be ok. But Frank had heard, through a friend of a friend, of a different kind of work up north.

Frank told George they should think about going to work in one of the lumber camps in the vast Huron Forest. He had heard that the work was rough but they pay was good; secretly Frank thought the hard work would be good for his young friends…it would turn them into men for sure. This was the first George had heard of the giant pines and the lumber industry to the north; he felt like it held great possibilities. The two old friends chatted for a few minutes more, and George said he had to be on his way.

After thanking Frankie for the advice, he turned and walked quickly down the street towards home. For some reason, he liked the idea. He mulled it over in his head and by the time he reached his front screen door, he had made up his mind to talk to Eddie about it.

Between Eddie and George, George was the leader. He had an easy time convincing Eddie that lumber was something they should look into. Frank put them in touch with a friend who worked on one of the lumber crews in the northern part of Lower Michigan; the friend assured them that two more young men would be a welcome addition to their crew any time. George and Eddie eagerly accepted the invitation to come up north and it was settled; they would start work on a lumber crew in early November.

Four months later George and Eddie got up at the crack of dawn, boarded a steamer docked in Detroit, and headed up river to Lake Huron. They grasped an old duffel bag each, their breath puffing out in front of them on deck in the cold morning air. They watched the only streets and sights they'd ever known drift away from them and finally disappear as the steamer picked up speed.

After a cold but uneventful cruise from Detroit, the chugging steamship pulled in to Oscoda, a small busy town situated where the Au Sable River spills into Lake Huron. The young men, slightly overwhelmed, left the swaying dock of the ship and trudged down to the end of the main street in the late afternoon chill, finding lodging in one of the small hotels in town. Though certainly attracted by the sights and sounds drifting out from the town saloons, it would be an early night for them; they had to report at the lumber camp in the forest far past the city limits not long after daybreak. They might have lingered a bit longer in their deep beds or around the fireplace that night if they'd known what the next few months had in store for them.

Next morning, George and Eddie found a ride without much difficulty with a horse and cart taking supplies to one of the camps in the forest. The driver whistled to his heavy plow horses and with a massive jerk that almost sent the two men tumbling off the back, the cart heaved off into the early morning darkness.

An hour and a half later, they stood at the edge of the lumber camp, wondering if this was the right place and listening with some regret to the sound of the horses' hooves clopping off in the distance and finally out of earshot. Looking around, the camp seemed empty. Shivering alone in the desolate, quiet cold of the morning, they realized they'd made it north.

Signs of recent habitation were everywhere however; booted footprints in the snow, the smell of bacon, a thin stream of smoke wisping up from a smoldering fire. Standing in the silence, they looked around and took it all in; the log cabins, the fire pits, the horse stable, the empty carts, the broken tools in a pile, extra heavy-duty chains under a tree.

"Helloooo!!!!" Eddie shouted nervously. They shivered and waited, listening, but heard nothing; their call echoed on and on deep into the forest. They ventured slowly into the camp, peeking into the crude cabins and tents. Already the cold and damp had seeped into their old boots they'd worn, and the wind was cutting through their thin city jackets they'd brought from home.

Gradually they became aware of the short puffing sounds of someone walking towards them out of the forest. Within minutes, a rough, broad-shouldered man appeared, closing the distance between them in giant strides. He wore thick old jeans, big ankle-high boots, a heavy coat and a furry hat made of beaver pulled down over his ears. His hands were shoved deep into the pockets of his flannel coat. His face was red from the cold.

He asked if they were the two from Detroit. He had a heavy Swedish accent, this man who had materialized from the trees and was as solid as any of the pine giants that stood nearby; he smelled like the dying fire and of the icy cold. He held out his hand and gruffly introduced himself as Nick, the boss, the Bull of the Woods. Their new boss doubtfully sized them up and down, seeming to disapprove. With a curt order to follow, he turned and began to crunch through the snow.

George and Eddie followed, running to keep up with him. They followed Nick into a dark and cold, crudely made log cabin. By the bunks and the clothes hanging on hooks along the wall, and the pervading smell of sweat, they knew they were in sleeping quarters. Nick pulled out boots, gloves, and jeans and told them they should get into town for warmer coats, and soon. He pointed to two bunks that were empty and told them to get used to their new beds. Turning to leave, he told the two friends they had five minutes to get their new things on and meet him back outside.

Sunlight shone and the wind whistled in through little chunks in the corners of the log cabin where the men had missed with mud. The two friends didn't say a word to each other as they fumbled in the dark with their ill-fitting but definitely warmer new boots and gloves. They were both greatly re-thinking their decision to come and work up north. However, it was much too late now to change their minds. They gamely stepped outside and found Nick, who, without a word, turned again and led them off down a snowy path towards the river.

George and Eddie put in their first twelve hours as lumbermen that day. The other men were friendly enough and showed them the ropes; they were glad for the new help. The two friends learned how to use an ax and a cross-cut saw, and how to work alone and with a partner. After an hour, they found they didn't notice the chilling cold anymore. As an hour turned to two, their muscles began to cry out, backs began to ache, toes to feel numb. They didn't dare complain as they watched these hardened lumbermen, or river rats as they were better known, hack and saw, push, drag, lift and load without a break or hitch. The daunting task of felling

120 foot high trees with 5 foot diameters and dragging them to the river's edge was all in a day's work to these men.

George and Eddie struggled greatly to keep up that first day, pushing themselves harder than they ever had in school or at their odd jobs back home. They walked back at the end of the line to the camp that evening limping, sore, cold and tired. They had forgotten which bunks were theirs and kicked off their boots and fell into the two remaining empty beds. They had just closed their eyes when they heard Gabriel the horn bellowing that it was 5:00 am, time to climb out of bed, still sore, and stumble outside for breakfast. They ate in the dark around a campfire, and at first sign of light were trudging down the path towards the river, following their new workmates and trying to keep up.

Days turned into weeks and months. Every day except Sunday was the same as the day before. Awakened by a bullhorn at 5am, they ate pancakes and biscuits with molasses, corned beef, doughnuts and fried potatoes and drank thick black strong coffee around a fire. Heads down, they marched off to where they had finished the night before, dragging their axes behind them, someone leading the horses that were hooked up to a massive hauling cart. At first sign of light they began to hack and saw, cutting the giant white pines into 16 foot logs and dragging them to the side of the river for the spring river run. By noon the cookees would show up with lunch, and they ate pea soup and re-heated breakfast crouching down in the snow or seated on tree stumps in silence; on the really cold days they ate huddled under blankets and ate their pies and cookies while warming their hands by a fire. Lunch lasted 30 minutes; it was a brief respite. Picking up their axes and saws with blistered hands, they worked until nightfall and the final sound of the bullhorn for that day. The walk back could be up to two miles; most of the men found room on the horse-drawn carts. Back at camp, the wet clothes and boots were hung up to dry in the bunkhouse, horses were brushed and stabled, axes were filed; the blacksmith could be heard beginning repairs on broken equipment. Shuffling off to the cook shanty, they sat down for another hot meal, this time meat and potatoes, biscuits and gravy, canned fruits and vegetables, hot pies and more coffee. They had 20 minutes to gulp down dinner, and no talking was allowed around the big, long heavy table. Back in the bunkhouse after dinner, the men either read or entertained each other with singing or tall tales. Lights out two hours later and the whole process started again at daybreak. At the end of the month, they were each given their $24.00.

Lumbering had proven to be hard work for George and Eddie. In the beginning, they questioned whether they could last the four months up here that they signed up for. But they got used to it, to the bitter cold, the long physical days, the same sights day in and out, and after a few weeks it all became routine.

Sunday was the only day the shanty boys had off; to a lumberman, Sundays were like gold. Six days a week these men worked their muscles sore in the icy forest hack-sawing, chopping, pulling, loading, dragging. They spent the vast majority of their day trying to keep warm, pulling hats down over ears and rubbing hands together. The physical work itself kept them warm; these men slept in the cold and worked in the cold.

So on Sundays, most of the men hitched rides into town for anything different to look at, anything different to eat. They shopped for supplies, picked up mail, and passed the time talking to the sawmill operators. They always ended up at one of the two boarding houses, drinking ale and playing cards in dark rooms with the local shopkeepers and traders. On Sundays, the lumber camps back in the forests would be silent and empty, except for the sounds of the horses munching and the cook making dinner.

George was different from the rest of the men. In spite of putting in his 12 hours a day in the cold, silent forest, ducking his head from the cold wintry wind, he was one of the few who did not go into town on Sundays.

On Sundays, George walked back into the woods towards the river, to the same spot he spent every other day of the week.

He didn't know when it happened; he only knew that one Sunday he felt like he wanted to escape *to* the forest, instead of escape *from* it like the rest of the men.

So George slept in on Sundays, lazily waking up to the sounds of the other men in different stages of their mornings. Sounds of the others drinking coffee around the fire, eating, talking, getting ready to head into town usually woke him up. George would sit up, rub the sleep from his eyes and wait patiently until the last of them had left the camp for town. He would comb his unruly hair with his fingers, pull on his heavy boots and coat and step outside into the empty camp.

He knew where he wanted to go. Hunching up his shoulders for the long walk, he followed the path the several miles to the river's edge. On Sundays he was completely alone; when the camp had disappeared from his view, he began to lose himself. After the long hard days he was working, he needed some quiet time, time to be by himself, time to think. George found that peace in the solitude of the wintry forest.

He had found a spot along the river that was high on a bluff, where the river made one of its graceful turns around a bend. The trees were thick here along the edge, and George was sheltered from the wind. He sat on a stump and got comfortable, breathing in the cold air that didn't seem to bother him anymore. He watched his breath come out in puffs and looked around him at the frozen, silent river below. The woods were devoid of all the usual noises; no men shouting, no hack saws grinding, no chains clinking. The bright red winter cardinals resumed their feeding as George settled in.

Sometimes it snowed on these Sundays, big giant flakes that froze to the bark of the trees; sometimes it was windy, other times still. George sat through it all, peacefully observing his new world. The bustling, noisy, dirty streets of Detroit were far away.

Hours later he came out of his trance, the biting cold finally getting to the tips of his fingers. He took one last, long gaze at the river and headed back into camp.

Winter turned into spring that year in the forest. With it came the thaw, when the log piles would be carefully floated down the river to the sawmills. The men who stayed and worked through spring made more money as the work became more dangerous; men sometimes lost their lives as the ice melted in huge lurching chunks and giant logs slipped and tumbled. Some of the men stayed for the log running; others took their leave and went home to families and friends, to be found next November checking in to their cabin and their bunk in the forest for another winter of lumbering.

George and Eddie had survived their first season as river rats. Eddie had made friends, and had discovered the comforts of the town pub. He liked the work but was looking forward to getting back to Detroit; he missed his mom's cooking and the smell of his father's cigars on a Sunday morning. Eddie was outgoing and loved a joke; he had become a favorite among the other men.

George was different; he had always been more of an introvert than Eddie. The others liked George; he was friendly but he was quiet, and kept to himself. He never made it into that tight-knit inner circle; men who were bound together by the camaraderie of a rowdy card game and big glasses of beer.

Talk around the camp at springtime always centered on who was going to stay for the spring thaw roll and who was leaving.

Eddie assumed George would be leaving with him soon, to head back south to Detroit. George had been giving this a lot of thought; he knew his friend would be disappointed with his decision. Not only had George decided to stay and help with the spring thaw river running, he knew he could never go back to living in the city. He needed to find a little home for himself, near the river. He knew he'd see his good friend next winter, but George had decided to stay up north for good.

****

The lumber era in Michigan lasted from the mid-1840s until the late 1910s. Forests were harvested for the white pine, which was made into homes, schools, and businesses. During that time, fortunes were made, land was surveyed and bought, tall tales grew, and a colorful history was forged. Many streets, schools, businesses and roads in the Oscoda area are named after prominent lumber barons of the era.

The famous Lumberman's Monument is a nine foot bronze statue, built in 1931 to memorialize the hundreds of hard-working young men who helped supply this young country with lumber for homes, schools, and offices. Many men even lost their lives in this line of work. The statue cost $50,000.00 to build, and portrays 3 men of the logging field: the sawyer with his ax and cross-cut saw, the river rat with his peavy, and the timber cruiser with his hand compass. The money to build the statue was collected from some of Michigan's principal lumber families, in the form of donations. The Monument sits off of East River Road, ten miles outside of Oscoda, in the Huron National Forest. There is a scenic overlook at the sight of the Monument, as well as a small souvenir shop for tourists and an interesting display of lumbermen artifacts, such as old pots and pans, worn out shoes, and rusted saws. A typical dinner has even been re-created on an old china plate. The Lumberman's Monument has become a popular stop for color-watchers, history buffs, and nature lovers who make the worthwhile trip to the Oscoda area.

CHAPTER THREE

Wurtsmith Air Force Base in Oscoda, MI was an integral part of the training of fighters for the Second World War; the era of World War II fighting squadrons is the stuff movies are made of. Lifelong friendships were made, lives saved and lost, atrocities committed, survival stories of hope and love told and retold. Fearless men and women both in the air and on the ground, daily sacrificed life and family to defend and protect U.S. soil and ideals. Rough and ready squadrons had names for their planes like Rae, Ramblin' Wreck, Hawkeye Gal, Birdie, Snorting Bull and Mommie. Even the famous all black Tuskegee Airmen trained at Wurtsmith for a time.

Though the drone and thrill of the sleek, precision fighting jets streaking across the Oscoda skies was silenced in 1993, there are small reminders that still exist to remind visitors of the once proud Air Force base that sprawled across the street from Lake Huron. Signs along the road still stand directing visitors to the base, as well as former Air Force housing and other structures that are slowly being assimilated into civilian use. The old base homes are now inhabited by Oscoda residents; a cargo airport continues to develop and operate out of the base; the Yankee Air Force Museum opens its doors to visitors daily, and Alpena Community College as well as a medical center have settled in on a portion of the 5200 acre field.

Today, this wartime history can be viewed in numerous aviation museums across the country. Squadron emblems can be bought on patches and posters on the internet. Countless books have been written, veterans interviewed, old black and white photos gazed at fondly. Oscoda will never forget the imposing presence of the steel gray Air Force planes resting on runways behind metal fences at Wurtsmith. As families wander along Lake Huron, eating ice cream and walking their dogs, they only have to look over their shoulders and across the road to see the barracks and hangars, sights they are still very proud of.

Jimmy, Caroline, and the River
mid 1940s

Caroline McGraw lounged in her favorite lawn chair under the stately old pecan tree, waiting for her husband Jimmy to get home from work. In her manicured hand was the latest novel she was reading, her finger stuck in the page to mark her place. Her trusty binoculars hung around her neck, ready in case she spotted a new bird she'd never seen before, or maybe a rare one that didn't make its appearance too often. This was Caroline's favorite part of the day, sitting in the heavy, sometimes sticky heat of an early Tennessee evening. She had on her coolest summer shorts, strappy sandals and sleeveless cotton shirt. She had made sure to put on her make-up again, fix her hair, and smooth out her smart summer clothes so she'd look fresh for Jimmy. She loved life, she loved her husband, and she loved her Tennessee.

Jimmy and Caroline had both been born and raised in Tennessee; it was the only home they'd ever known. Caroline came from old, genteel money, and James was very smart with the managing of it; the young couple had managed to bear the brunt of the depression better than most young couples their age. They felt fortunate to have a small, airy house with a screened-in porch, food on the table, the old pecan tree, and each other. The economy was finally showing signs of turning around in 1939... surely the upcoming year would bring prosperity and happiness with it.

James McGraw was a young, up and coming pilot in the United States Air Force. He was being trained to fly the new P-47 Thunderbolt, the most advanced fighting machine of its time. It was becoming widely assumed that the United States would soon become involved in the European War; Jimmy knew his responsibility as a fighter pilot and was up to the task. He loved his job, his wife, and his country.

When he got to work that morning, Jimmy was told his commanding officer needed to see him, on a matter of some importance. Jimmy got the news that he was being stationed at the Air Force base in Oscoda, Michigan, known as Wurtsmith. A squadron of P-47 fighters was being assembled; they were to begin their training immediately at Wurtsmith. For Jimmy, this re-positioning was a part of his job, and the commitment he'd made to his country. He knew however, that it would be a very difficult thing to tell Caroline. He dreaded coming home that night to tell her, knowing how she loved her home and the mountains and lush rolling hills of Tennessee.

Caroline pushed herself out of her chair and ran to meet him as Jimmy pulled in their narrow driveway that evening. He gave her his usual little squeeze and kiss on the cheek, which she lovingly returned. She smiled her winning smile and beamed up at him with the usual question, "how was your day, darling?" Jimmy smiled gamely and wondered how he could possibly keep the news from her, even for a few minutes. He decided to just get it over with, and turned towards the house. Once inside, Jimmy broke the news to his wife as gently as possible.

Caroline loved and supported her Jimmy in everything, but this was almost too much to bear. Leave Tennessee for Michigan?? For *Oscoda, Michigan??*

"Isn't it just icy and bitterly cold there, most of the time??" she asked in desperation. She thought of her beloved pecan trees, of the yellow tulip trees and the plum trees, the persimmons and poplars that she loved, and knew she could never be happy in Michigan. Jimmy did his best to make his wife feel better. "I've heard it can be real nice there in the summertime, Carrie. They have beautiful lakes and rivers, and lots of open country, and well, birds, they have birds there too."

He knew that sounded weak to his wife, but he did the best he could. Caroline gradually came to accept the idea of moving to Michigan - what choice did she have? - and a month later they loaded up the Ford and started the drive north.

The move went smoothly enough. Jimmy knew Caroline was deeply upset about having to move, but he also knew she was doing her best to be positive about it. For that, he was grateful. They settled into their small home on base; the small row houses that all looked the same were nothing like their little brick home with the pecan trees down south, but still, they had each other.

After the initial upheaval of the move and the adjustment to a new job and new surroundings, Jimmy's days quickly went back to being routine. He was fascinated by the new plane he'd be flying, the new squadron that was being formed. He loved everything about his new job; he threw himself into his work. As the war loomed ever closer, so did Jimmy's dedication to his commander and squadron. Jimmy's mind had more than enough things to be occupied with.

Caroline, on the other hand, was despondent. She had tried hard to be optimistic about the move to Michigan, but once the activities of moving, and moving in, and getting accustomed to the area had died down, she found herself alone most of the time in a small barrack-like house. She hated it here; she hated Oscoda. She could not force herself to make friends or get excited about anything. She cried during the day when Jimmy was at work, but still did her best to be fresh and happy when Jimmy got home in the evenings. In spite of Jimmy being wrapped up in the new challenges at work, he knew Caroline well and knew she was not happy. He decided to make it a priority to figure out a way to lift her spirits.

When his mind wasn't completely focused on his work, Jimmy thought long and hard about how to cheer up his wife. He knew the thing that made her happiest was being outside in nature, either walking in it, swimming in it, driving in it, whatever. Caroline had so enjoyed long walks through the hills in Tennessee, swimming in a lazy river, or just being outside swinging in the hammock and breathing in the musky evening smells.

Jimmy left work early one day, with an idea in mind.

Caroline jumped up from her armchair, where she'd been sitting crying. She thought she'd heard Jimmy's car pull up. She ran to the window, her heart pounding. What was Jimmy doing home so early?? In a panic she ran into the bathroom and splashed water on her face, cleaned up her running make-up, and fluffed up her hair. She dried her face and stepped out of the bathroom with a forced smile as Jimmy walked in the front door. "Hey sweetie! Surprised??" Jimmy asked cheerfully.

"Hello, darling", Caroline said, trying to look happy. "How come you're home so early?"

"We had the option of leaving a little early today, so I jumped on it. How was your day?"

Caroline lied and said her day was great, but she couldn't look him in the eye. There was an awkward pause as Jimmy slid off his shoes. "Hey Carrie, did you know Lake Huron is practically right across the street? Well, I was thinking, it's such a gorgeous day outside, why don't we take a walk down by the lake?"

Caroline couldn't have been less thrilled. She methodically made her way into the bedroom to put on her tennis shoes and sweater. Jimmy changed out of his work clothes, grabbed a cookie and the house keys, and they stepped outside into the bright afternoon sunshine.

It really was just a short drive, up the road and across the street, to the sandy beaches of Lake Huron. Caroline's perfect hair was whipped across her face by the lake wind as she stepped out of the car. She pulled her sweater closer to her as Jimmy smiled down at her and put his arm around her. They followed the narrow sandy path through the evergreens down to the beach. Coming out of the woods, Lake Huron spread out before them, as far as their eyes could see, in three directions. Caroline was a little taken aback at the vastness of it, at the coolness of the temperature, even in the late Michigan summer, and the driftwood dripping with seaweed. This was certainly like no lake she had ever seen. Other couples and retired people walked slowly up and down the welcoming beach, some dipping their feet in the teasing waves and others just letting their bare feet crunch through the dry sand. It really was a beautiful, quiet afternoon. Jimmy gently guided Caroline towards the water, then they turned their way south and headed down the beach. Seagulls flew over them, landing, picking at the dead fish; some bobbed in the water and let the waves bring them in to shore. Jimmy leaned down and kissed Caroline on her temple, and she looked up at him and smiled. They walked, with Jimmy's arm around her, slowly down the beach. The air was fresh, the beach peaceful. The waves pounded the shore. They didn't say much, just kept ambling, until the sun began to sink and the air turned a little chill; they turned around and lazily headed back towards the car.

Over the next few days, Jimmy thought that Caroline's spirits seemed to have lifted a little, but he couldn't be sure. He knew she enjoyed the afternoon at the lake. In truth, Caroline did enjoy the day at the lake, but she wasn't used to such a lake as Lake Huron, where the wind blew fiercely, where the temperature dropped 10 degrees, where fish bones and seaweed littered the shore. She was not immune though to the calming, relaxing, gentle rolling of the waves to the shore, of the hot sand filtering through her toes, of the lazy feeling one gets just walking endlessly with no idea of time. It dawned on her a few days later what the afternoon at the lake had been all about: Jimmy's attempt to lift her out of the little rut she constantly lived in these days. That sunny afternoon on the beach had been the best afternoon she'd had since they got to Michigan. She wanted so badly to feel good again, to be happy, and to not have to force her smile for her husband every night when he came home from work.

The next morning Caroline finished up the breakfast dishes and peeked her head outside to see what kind of a day it was going to be. The sun was shining in a clear, bright blue Michigan sky. She opened the curtains to let some of that sunshine into the small living room. For the first time since they moved here, she did not feel like immediately slouching in her chair and wasting the day away. She pulled on some loose pants, slipped on her tennis shoes, and pulled her short bouncy hair back into a clasp. Grabbing her sweater, blanket, book, and binoculars, she walked the short ¼ mile up the road to the path to the lake. This time, she was ready for the wind; it even felt good to her. She found a spot on the beach in the sun and spread her blanket out. Caroline lie there reading for two hours before drifting off, her face pressed into the plaid blanket, the sun warming her to her bones and the wind softly caressing her as she faded in and out in a luscious, timeless sleep.

When she woke suddenly, she realized she'd been at the lake for almost 4 hours. Groggy, she glanced quickly at her watch and realized if she didn't hurry, she wouldn't have time to get Jimmy his dinner before he got home. She jumped up still in a sleepy daze, grabbed her things, and walked as fast as she could down the path towards the road that led to home. She didn't realize until she was almost done cooking dinner that she felt calm and peaceful and not sad, for the first time in a long while.

The next few days were spent in the same way, reading at the beach. It happened very fast; by the second day, she had come to look forward to getting out of bed again. Jimmy was amazed at the difference in his wife; amazed and relieved. He knew she had been spending her days down by the water. The color had come back to those beautiful cheeks, the spring back in her step. It was almost as if she couldn't wait for him to finish breakfast in the morning so she could send him off to work and go to the lake. Caroline had come alive again.

Friday morning was like no other; Jimmy left, and Caroline took off for the lake. She knew today had to be a short day though; Friday was her day to clean house. She spread her blanket out in her favorite spot by the shore and had just settled down to read when a couple she'd been saying hi to every day walked by and waved. She waved back, as usual. This time though, they shyly approached her instead of walking by. They turned out to be a sweet old couple, who'd retired up here in one of the tiny beach houses that hugged the shoreline. They wanted to introduce themselves, as they'd been seeing Caroline every day now for the past two weeks. She told them that she and her husband were new to town, Jimmy having been stationed at Wurtsmith for training.

The old couple asked her how she enjoyed the lake; "I love it" she said with eager enthusiasm, really meaning it. They asked her if she and her husband had been to the river yet.

"What river?" Caroline asked, squinting up at them, intrigued.

The old couple looked at each other and smiled. "The Au Sable, of course. It's the most beautiful thing you'll ever see. You and your hubby should really take a drive down there. It's just down that road, not too far. Try and do it before the summer's over, really dear." They turned to continue on their daily walk down the beach, Caroline thanking them for the suggestion as they walked off. She picked up her book with a contented smile and tried to read, but her mind kept wandering to the idea of a river so close by.

That night after dinner, Caroline asked Jimmy about going to the Au Sable. Jimmy could not get over the change in his wife; things were so much happier at home now that Caroline was getting back to her cheerful self.

Jimmy promised her he would find out from someone on base how to get to the river. It was a unanimous decision to drive and see it that weekend.

Saturday morning came and Caroline was out of bed before Jimmy. He had found out from a fellow pilot that the best way to see the Au Sable was by canoe. They'd done some canoeing back in Tennessee, and they both loved it. There were several tiny shacks to rent canoes from along River Road as they got closer to the river. They stopped at one and soon drove off with a canoe strapped on top of their car.

The dirt road took them west, deep into the heart of the Huron forest. With the windows rolled down and dust kicking up around them, Jimmy and Caroline were like two teen-agers that day, laughing, joking, and teasing each other all the way to the river. As the sandy bumpy road took them closer to the river, it began to twist and turn, coming close enough and giving them their first glimpse of the river off to their left. The morning sun made the deep blue river sparkle, as if someone had spilled hundreds of tiny twinkling diamonds onto its surface. The air around them was crisp with the enticing, deep scent of evergreen; they sat up straight and inhaled huge breaths of the forest air.

After finding a good place to stop, park, and put the canoe in the river, the couple got the cumbersome boat off the top of the car with little difficulty. Caroline had brought her sweater and her binoculars; Jimmy, a cooler filled with sandwiches and sodas. They waded out knee deep into the slow-moving river, pushing the canoe ahead of them. Jimmy signaled to Caroline she should get in the boat, so she hopped in. Jimmy followed a second later, picked up his paddle, and they were off. Neither one of them ever having been to the river before, they had no idea what to expect. They were simply hoping for a lovely day on a pretty river.

After the momentary rush of keeping the boat stabilized and making sure all things they brought were on board and dry, they got into a rhythm of dipping their paddles completely in unison. Their canoe glided silently down the middle of the gently winding river. Out on the river, the air smelled of sand and warm sun, the gentle breeze bringing the scent of sumac and dry grass. They were surrounded on both sides by dense forests of evergreen, birch, and maples; Caroline's imagination wandered and she created stories for all the tiny inlets along the shore. The sky was a light blue that day, with a few wispy cotton candy clouds for contrast. The wind rustling the birch leaves was the only sound they heard that still morning, that and the soft plunking sound of their paddles dipping in and out of the clear, wide river. The fish were jumping that day too, Jimmy and Caroline exclaiming at each silver body flashing momentarily out of the water. They were taking in their surroundings, in their own way. They both loved the quiet serenity of this gentle giant river, majestically and calmly twisting its way through the Huron forest. Caroline shook her head and squinted up into the sun, letting it warm her as she relaxed her paddle on her knees.

They had hardly spoken a word to each other several hours later, each in their own world as they drifted slowly down the river. Jimmy broke the silence by inquiring about a peanut butter and jelly sandwich; Caroline was getting hungry too and passed one to Jimmy and a grape soda, too. They let the canoe drift along, the slow tide carrying them down the river and towards one shore.

Caroline's eyes and ears automatically focused on the approaching shoreline. She had been an avid birdwatcher for most of her life, and her sharp eyes were often trained on the trees and skies. Her body straightened a little as she saw something flickering through the pine trees. She fumbled for her binoculars and snapped them to her eyes, focusing as she searched. Caroline had done a little homework before coming on this canoe trip; she had read about the endangered Kirtland's Warbler that nested only in northern Michigan, and was keen to see one. She knew what to look for: yellow breast, blue-gray feathers, and loud lilting song. She followed something small through the branches before it flew away; was that a warbler? She could not be sure. Caroline kept her binoculars glued to her eyes for a few more minutes, letting Jimmy steer the canoe. With no more movement in the trees, she turned back to the river.

"Did you see something?" Jimmy asked his wife.

"I'm not sure", she said softly.

Caroline picked up her paddle again and looked at the sky; the sun had reached its peak and then some.

She sighed and closed her eyes, hanging on to that moment in the sun. Neither one of them wanted to think about turning around and heading back down the dirt road towards home. So, they didn't. At least, not right away. The two of them let the river take them for awhile longer, before turning the canoe around and dipping their paddles towards home.

Jimmy and Caroline would always remember their first day at the river, the day spent in the warm sun, the smell of the sandy shore and the summer breezes around every bend. Caroline wasn't sure if she'd seen the warbler that day, but she knew that she'd be looking again the next time they made the trip to the Au Sable.

****

Wurtsmith Air Force Base became an important training ground for squadrons of P-47s in the early 1940s. The P-47 was used in World War II and was considered an advanced bomber for its time. In 1960, Wurtsmith became part of Strategic Air Command, set up to respond to possible nuclear attack by the Soviet Union. In 1965, pilots began training in B52s, and began flying missions in Southeast Asia. B52 training continued at Wurtsmith well into the late 1980s. During the '70s and '80s, the squadrons training at the base earned many awards for readiness and performance. Squadrons from Wurtsmith were still being sent on missions around the world up to 1990. It was in 1991 that, due to the end of the cold war and budget woes, Congress approved the closure of more than 30 military bases, Wurtsmith being one of them. Wurtsmith was officially closed on June 30, 1993. The economy of Oscoda suffered greatly from the base closure, and is still struggling to counter the bad side effects of losing over three thousand jobs. A new industrial park has sprung up in its place and is slowly bringing life back to the small, lakeside town of Oscoda.

****

The Kirtland's Warbler, once considered highly endangered with only a few hundred birds existing, is making a positive comeback thanks to careful behavior study and preservation efforts. This small, beautiful songbird winters in the Bahamas and the males fly back to northern Michigan in May to begin the mating season. The females follow shortly after and the courtships begin. The Kirtland's Warbler nearly died out due to its very specific reproduction requirements; they nest only under Jack Pines and require fairly large habitats per mating pair. The weather and soil condition, and even the age of the Pines themselves have to be exact or the birds do not mate and produce with success. Because they nest on the ground, their nests are easy prey for other "parasitical" birds, which lay their eggs in the Warbler nests; when the young chicks hatch, the larger birds out-muscle the smaller Warbler chicks for food and care, dramatically reducing the survival rate of the Warbler young.

In 1976 a Kirtland's Warbler Recovery Plan was launched, and thanks to the cooperation of several agencies including the Michigan Department of Natural Resources and the U.S. Fish and Wildlife Service, the parasite birds are being controlled, the Jack Pine stands are being carefully managed and the Warbler's habitat is closely monitored and protected. A count in 2002 showed over 1000 males and evidence has been found of Kirtland's Warblers in Wisconsin, Ontario and Quebec.

****

Canoeing on the Au Sable has developed into a national affair; what started as a gentle, relaxing way to spend an afternoon has morphed for some into a yearly sporting event, the start of which is attended by more people than any other event in Northern Michigan. July 23, 2010 will see the 63rd running of the Au Sable River Canoe Marathon, which starts in Grayling, ends in Oscoda, lasts for up to 20 hours, 120 miles, and tempts participants with more than $50,000.00 in cash and prizes. It is the longest non-stop canoe race in North America. The Canoer's Memorial was erected along a stretch of the River Road Scenic Byway, overlooking the river, and is dedicated to the thousands of hardy canoers who tackle the overnight canoe marathon each year.

The Au Sable draws hundreds of casual canoers each year as well. This 140 mile river is renowned for its beauty, accessibility, and clean, clear water. The fall color change along the Au Sable is not to be missed; people travel from all over the world to experience the striking vistas of the trees along the river as they transform themselves every year into reds, burgundies, oranges, and yellows before finally losing all their leaves as winter closes in.

Au Sable River

PART TWO

THREE SMALL ROOMS,
A WELL, PUMP AND
AN OUTHOUSE

THE CABIN IS BUILT

Being Built (Jack Causgrove looks on)

THE HALES
Cliff and Helen

Clifford Rosswell and Helen Countess Hale began their married life together by buying a two-story house. They bought it in Bay City, Michigan, a modest town on picturesque Saginaw Bay, tucked in the curve of the thumb that is the Michigan mitten. Cliff and Helen were just two of generations of German Hales who had settled in the area; by the 1900's, Germans represented the highest ethnic percentage of this little city on Saginaw Bay, and the same still holds true today.

This relatively quiet, small town with a river running through it has an interesting history, shaped entirely by the vast, seemingly endless stretches of Michigan forests, covering most of the area to the north of it.

In fact, Bay City exists today because of the great White Pine.

In the days before European settlement, what is now Bay City was the preferred camping ground of the Chippewa Indians. In addition to the abundant game and fertile soil, Native Americans settled there because of the proximity to the Saginaw River trading routes and beyond, to Saginaw Bay and Lake Huron. The Chippewa thrived there for generations, aggressively defending their Bay and trading routes.

For the same geographical reasons the Native Americans chose to settle there, rough and rugged pioneer Leon Tromble built the area's first house on the banks of the Saginaw River in the early 1800s. Tromble's small log hut soon drew his entrepreneurial nephews Joseph and Mador to the area, who in 1835 established the first trading post along the river; this rustic log trading post also doubled as the town's first hotel, providing guests could supply their own bedrolls.

The next 10 years saw the arrival of more settlers to the river and to the vast pine forests to the north in Bay County; soon another hotel and trading post sprung up.

The Midwest's lust for finished lumber could not be denied. In 1844 lumber production came to the county with a rush and the first mill was constructed at the mouth of the winding Kawkawlin River. Lumber quickly became king, output increasing in leaps and bounds as the need for homes and schools grew. The budding shipping industry demanded it to power their hulking ships transporting goods across the Great Lakes. At the height of the lumber boom, around 1875, more than 50 mills operated in the area; the population continued to grow and commerce increased. Bay City was beginning to bustle.

By the turn of the century the endless thick forests of the north actually began to thin out from all the intense logging; steel production and boat building slowly took over and pushed out the lumber yards. For survival's sake, Bay County adjusted to the changes, its shipyards producing a large variety of craft including U.S Destroyers and missile vessels for the Australian Navy, and even luxury yachts for the Kennedys in the 1960's.

Over the years, the building of naval and commercial steel watercraft shifted to the production of recreational boats, including sailboats, catamarans and iceboats; one small company in Bay County has produced more Gold Cup champion hydroplanes than any other single builder nationwide.

Today, Bay City is a medium-sized town with a small town feel. The Saginaw River winds its way through the city, past old-time hardware stores and modern office buildings. To get anywhere in the downtown area, you cross the river at least once on one of the many bridges throughout the city. Beyond the downtown area the bookstores and fabric shops give way to charming quiet streets, lined with older wood houses with wide front porches and huge oak trees in the front yards. The lawns are neat and trimmed, flags fly from metal porch hitches, and brightly colored flowers sway from window flowerboxes during the summer months.

In the 1920's, Cliff and Helen moved to one of those quiet streets and in to one of those quaint wooden houses. The front porch steps were deep and wide, and the fading pale green paint was always peeling. Helen cooked everything in a big simmering pot and Cliff worked hard during the week managing a hardware store; he worked in his backyard garden on the weekends. All of the vegetables that Helen served on her big heavy wooden table in the sunny dining room came from Cliff's neat and well-tended garden.

Cliff and Helen Hale

They were quiet, unassuming people. Helen was sweet, caring, and deeply devoted to Cliff, who in turn loved Helen and was a good, honest provider. They raised four beautiful daughters in that house on South Chilson, who grew up and had professional careers, then married and filled that white wood house with grandchildren. As their hair turned gray and their lives slowed down, Cliff and Helen loved those visits from the grandkids the most; their days as grandparents rounded out a happy, fulfilling life the two had shared together.

Looking back to when I was an energetic little girl in the early '70s, hopping up those deep wooden porch steps to see Grandma Hale, my memories may be very similar to the Hale daughters'. Except Grandma was older and often simply sitting in her big easy chair waiting for me, and sadly Grandpa had passed away. The big front door was always open for us; I don't remember ever having to open the door to get inside. The dining room was still sunny and still had the same crocheted table cloth covering the wood table. My favorite stuffed animal would be sitting in a chair waiting for me, a big, faded homemade hound dog named Droopy. I used to run to Droopy first and then straight into Grandma's lap. Grandma didn't keep up the vegetable garden after Grandpa died, but she did tend her beautiful purple and pink flowers that wound around ornate wooden trellises in the back yard. We'd always make our way out into the bright back yard to sit and swing in the sun, passing through the kitchen with its crooked wooden floor and simmering pot of stew.

I can remember being a little scared of the upstairs rooms at Grandma's house for some childish reason, where my mom and her sisters had their bedrooms growing up. Maybe it was because downstairs was so warm and welcoming and the upstairs rooms where I slept were colder with not a lot of sun. Very little light made it up to the small second floor, and the tiny windows were completely covered by the branches of the huge oak tree. Next morning after spending a night upstairs, I would wake up early, jump out of the big, creaking antique bed and run downstairs, looking for Grandma. It didn't matter how early I'd come running down those steps in the morning; Grandma was always up already, wrapped in her robe and with her hair covered with a gauzy net, usually in the kitchen. She'd stop what she was doing when she'd see me come downstairs, and sit in her chair so I could climb in her lap and snuggle with her. The uneasy memories of the night I'd spent upstairs would fade as the morning sun streamed in the front windows. What I remember most about Grandma Hale is her gingham dresses, her black heavy shoes, and the way she always called me "honey".

The Hale house on Chilson Street

Young Cliff Hale was certainly a man who counted his blessings. In the mid 1940's, he had a small, neat home; he had a wife he loved dearly and four beautiful daughters. He had a good, secure job and free time to spend in his garden out back. He was able to pay his bills, with just a little

38

left over each month. Content as he was, he had always wanted one more thing though, and that was a place where he could go and hunt during hunting season.

Cliff Hale

Cliff worked hard at the hardware store and had a passion for hunting; he and his friends went to the wilds of northern Michigan to hunt deer whenever they could. At that time, his oldest daughter Shirley was twenty-one years old, his youngest Janie was six, with Pat and Bobby in between. Cliff knew he had a big family depending on him, but he could not put the thought of building his own hunting cabin out of his mind.

Helen Hale camping out

He knew it might be a bit of a risk, but Cliff simply could not ignore his dream any longer. After months of careful thought, discussion, and planning, Cliff Hale and family friend Jack Thomas took the plunge, pooled their savings and bought a small piece of land together, deep in the Huron Forest.

Roughly ninety miles north of Bay City is a remarkable river that snakes and cuts its way through the woods and ends at Lake Huron. In 1945, the Huron Forest along the Au Sable River stretched for miles and miles, unmarked by civilization, almost untouched by modern man. The forests were deep and thick and teemed with deer, skunks, raccoons and rabbits, black bear and countless game birds and song birds. This was exactly the kind of place Cliff and Jack had wanted to find; a hunter's paradise.

Their dream was a simple one: to build a small, very basic cabin that would serve as a shelter for them after a long day out hunting in the cold woods. They only wanted it to have four walls and a roof, some sort of stove for heat, a dining room table, and two bedrooms with soft, comfortable beds. They didn't want frills or luxury; they wanted a quiet place with no one else around where both men and their families could go and hunt, and then hang their wet and frosty gloves and hats to dry when the day was done. Their plans were no grander than a small, square, log cabin in the woods.

They hired Helen's Uncle Bill to build the cabin. Uncle Bill was not a builder, but simply a man with a little time to spare who was good with his hands. After Bill enlisted the help of friend and Cooke Dam operator Art Clement, he hauled an old trailer up to the new triangular piece of property near the Au Sable and began to clear the small plot of land in the summer of 1945. Cliff's dream was finally in the making.

Building the cabin was long, hard work for this generous uncle and friend. Their plot of land was a thick, almost impenetrable tangle of forest, with an uneven floor and dense undergrowth. Simply clearing the land would be Bill's first challenge. At the time, the only other signs of human life up there were the men who lived and worked 1/2 mile down the rough dirt road at Cooke Dam, one of six newly constructed hydroelectric plants along the 140 mile Au Sable River. Fortunately, northern Michigan summers are beautiful, with warm days and cool nights; Bill had the weather in his favor.

Uncle Bill and Art's metal axes rang out sharply in the otherwise silent forest as they chopped and felled, then dragged away the giant scented pine trees. The trailer where Bill stored their equipment also doubled as his home for that summer, where he would stretch out in the dark silence of night, exhausted from the physical work he'd done each day. Wild animal sounds lulled him off to sleep, in the safety of his rusted home on wheels.

Wanting to lend their hands, Cliff and his friend Jack Thomas made the ninety mile drive up to the forest where Uncle Bill and Art were building, on the weekends and whenever they could get away from their jobs. Sometimes they brought friends and family willing to pitch in on this labor of love; they always brought their newest member of the family, a small, excited Jack Russell Terrier mix named Cookie. Cookie was the very first of many Hale family pets to hang out of the car window, whimpering in excitement as the smells of the forests closed in, as they neared the turnoff to the cabin. This small little spotted dog, memorialized forever in tiny black and white crackled photos thumb-tacked to the cabin walls, could not have known the canine tradition she was starting as she panted and pawed at the windows of the family station wagon heading up north.

Driving up north

Cliff, Jack, their families, and Cookie drove up north as often as they could to help out Uncle Bill that summer. From the first swings of the ax, to a little clearing in the woods, to holes filled in and a frame constructed, their cabin was taking shape. Next came hills of sawdust, piles of timber, discarded, bent nails and the outlines of two bedrooms. The walls and ceilings were next and finally the finishing touches; the screen doors, the hand pump out front, and the outhouse out back.

As it was to be his cabin, Cliff wanted to inspect every stage of the building of it. He was the first person out of the car when they arrived at their grassy lot up north and, friendly greetings over between him and Bill, he walked over to his cabin and began to take a sometimes critical look around. He pushed his sleeves back and stepped up onto the dusty floorboards; he grasped a few supports and jerked them to make sure they'd hold. He glanced around the emerging floor plan and ran his fingers through his hair, imagining where he'd hang his gun and where he'd play cards at night. On many visits, he shoved back his hat, pointed to a board or two and commented to Uncle Bill, "These boards aren't straight". Bill was not concerned. He glanced at the boards, wiped the sweat off his brow and, shrugging his shoulders carelessly reminded Cliff "well, it's good enough for you".

Cliff kept up the occasional critiques, and Bill kept delivering the same reply. It was a cabin being built among friends, and Bill knew his work would hold, that the boards were straight and the supports solid. Cliff would then pick up a hammer and the men would begin to work side by side in the hot Michigan sun.

The finished product, a manly 900 square foot cabin, was completed as the summer of 1945 dwindled to a balmy close in late September. This true log cabin had three rooms in total. The main large room served as a sitting room, kitchen, and dining area. The sitting area was filled with old overstuffed rocking chairs and couches that no one wanted at their homes back in town. The kitchen table was a large oval big enough to fit eight sturdy wood chairs comfortably around. The kitchen cabinets were built up to the ceiling and filled over time with cracked old china plates and cups that were designated "cabin cups" as soon as they'd chip at home. The cabin was heated with a square version of an oil fueled pot-bellied stove, which could heat up the small new cabin tremendously while still set on "low". An old ice box was purchased and brought up; electricity had not yet made its way that deep in the forest. Uncle Bill rounded out his building projects by constructing two double bunk beds, one for each of the bedrooms. Matching wooden ladders were built for each bunk bed, and striped wool Hudson's Bay blankets and thick white feather ticks were bought for warmth at night. By the time the building was done, the two families didn't have a lot of money left to put into the cabin, so they put thin black tar paper down on the floors and the two wives, Helen Hale and Agnes Thomas, decorated the inside with old photos, fresh paint and worn out knick-knacks from their homes. There was no indoor plumbing; a deep hole was dug outside on one side of the cabin and a hand pump was installed for fresh water. A wooden outhouse was built a discreet 30 feet to the rear of the cabin, the path to the outhouse lined with white birch logs so it could better be seen at night. With all the driving to and from the cabin site, a road of sorts had been worn leading up to the cabin. Bill had cleared only enough trees to make room for the little structure; the cabin was nestled into the pine and birch trees, which surrounded it like a cocoon. The view from every window was dark green evergreens, peeling white birch, and deep blue sky.

Helen Hale at the cabin

Cliff and Jack's dream hunting cabin finally seemed finished; they could start using it that November. Helen and Agnes had had an idea of their own, and to add to the womanly touches they had already made to the inside of the cabin, they had gone into town and hired a woodworker to carve out the 18 inch wide wooden sign that is still nailed to the front of the cabin today. They brought it back and unveiled it to the men, who hung it up above the two front windows. They all stepped outside their new cabin with the grass up to their knees, the leaves starting to turn, and arm-in-arm, tilted their heads to read the newly hung sign:

GOODNUFRUS

THE HALE SISTERS

I noticed something one October about 8 years ago, when a gathering of some of the women in the extended Hale family were up north at the cabin for our annual big Girls Weekend. This weekend event started about fifteen years ago; those of us who can make it meet up north at the cabin when the colors along the river are at their peak. We drive up there with sleeping bags and cots, and are prepared to sleep on the couch or even floor if necessary. We sit around and do absolutely nothing except drink coffee, take walks, laugh about old times, play board games, cook, and eat.

I was standing in the cabin kitchen on one of these girl weekends, cutting tomatoes for a salad. My mom and her three sisters were sipping hot chocolate in the living room, laughing loudly and chatting with cousins and nieces.

It was then that I noticed it; with my back turned, it was impossible to tell which sister was talking, all four of them sounded so much the same. Their laughter, intonations, and phrases all sounded identical to each other. These wonderful four sisters who shared so much growing up, still shared everything, long after they had each gotten married and moved out across the state of Michigan. They had lived their lives so differently, but the love they felt for family and their little log cabin in the woods always bound them together.

Photo at the cabin: Janie, Bobby, Pat, Shirley

Shirley Hale

Shirley Hale

In 1924, Americans ate Wheaties and enjoyed Dum Dum suckers for the first time; Gershwin's breathtaking *Rhapsody in Blue* was presented to an adoring public; and on August 28, the first of four daughters for Clifford Roswell and Helen Countess Hale was born. Being the first, Shirley Helen got her own bedroom in the upstairs rooms.

Helen doted on Shirley, their first born. She had light brown hair and dark eyebrows; the first of four striking young Hale women. Her childhood was spent playing with her younger sister Pat, playing with friends, riding the bus to the local schools, and learning how to be prudent as the Depression settled in.

Shirley grew up to be a perfect blend of Cliff and Helen. From Cliff, she got his quiet determination and iron will. From Helen came sweetness, compassion, and kindness. Being the oldest, she shared a special bond with her parents, and when Shirley graduated from Central High School, entered Bay City Business College and moved out of the house, Cliff and Helen were sad to see her go.

By the time Cliff and Helen started thinking about building a cabin, Shirley was newly married to Jack Causgrove, the love of her life. She had met Jack at business school; he was studying to be a CPA. Jack and Shirley were building a small house of their own and had their own concerns and things that took up a lot of their time; they were only mildly interested in the construction of the hunting cabin. She was happy for her father, knowing how he loved to hunt in the northern Michigan forests. She imagined she'd make it up to the new cabin someday, and probably occasionally after that, if she and Jack had time.

With the arrival of her first born son Johnny in 1948, Shirley's world became one of diapers, games for little boys, and staying at home while Jack worked. She listened to her dad talk about the new cabin, about the endless, deep woods, and the quiet, silvery snowfalls up north. To her, it was a man's hunting cabin and not much more.

The summer after Shirley's son was born, Cliff and Helen decided they needed to make a special trip up north to their cabin to make a few minor repairs. Up to this point, the cabin had been used strictly for the purpose it was built for, during early winter for hunting. Eleven months out of the year, the cabin was winterized, oil cut off to the stove, doors locked and curtains closed. Cliff had badly wanted his oldest daughter to see his new place up north, which he was very proud of; he already had fond memories of the place. He and Helen talked Shirley and Jack into taking a day or two off and driving up to the cabin with them, one beautiful summer weekend. The five of them, and Cookie the dog, drove up together. Shirley, loaded up with baby bags and bottles, was looking forward to time spent with the four favorite people in her life.

The first thing they did when they got to the cabin was pull back all the curtains and open all the windows, letting in the warm breezes and the smells of the forest. Shirley took her first steps inside this little cabin she'd heard so much about. It seemed a little dark at first, but with the windows now open, the warm breeze began to drift in as the sun filtered through the dusty windows. The rustic rooms filled with the scent of pine.

Jack and Shirley got their choice of bedrooms and made up their beds.

Johnny's toys were brought out and Cookie raced around outside, sniffing out animal holes and digging where necessary. This funny little spunky dog's favorite and unexplainable northern pastime was to find any rock she could get her mouth around and drag it round to the front of the cabin, leaving it near the front door. Helen's job was to get a quick lunch ready, so she set out her grocery bags on the long cupboard and started on a lunch of salami sandwiches, with vegetables from the garden at home to munch on. Shirley sat in her shorts and t-shirt on the edge of the long, torn couch, watching Johnny play on the round, rough-knit rug in the center of the living room. She looked around at the sparse but homey rooms, taking it all in. It was warmer than she'd thought it would be, more welcoming. On the road in, they had driven along the scenic Au Sable for a mile or so; Shirley asked if they could take a walk down to the river in the afternoon.

After lunch, the two families put on tennis shoes and on that warm afternoon Shirley took her first of what would be countless walks down to the Au Sable. The place they stopped that day so many years ago is the same sunny place we all still walk to; because of Cooke Dam half mile down the road, the river is deep, very wide, and slow-moving; the clearing in the trees makes the water accessible. They took Johnny's little shoes off at that soft sandy spot, and he waded in up to his knees, kicking up waves and grabbing at round, polished stones. Minutes turned into hours as Jack and Shirley, Cliff and Helen watched Johnny and Cookie play in the river, and took turns wandering up and down the small bluffs and paths along the banks. Shirley knew by looking at Jack's face that he loved it up there.

Minor cabin repairs for the time forgotten, the little party by the river let the day drift by, lazing in the sun and sand until they started getting hungry for dinner. Johnny had exhausted himself, falling asleep in Shirley's lap; Cookie sat panting next to Cliff. They stood up, wiped the sand from their shorts and walked up the little hill to the dirt road. As they rounded the slight bend in the grassy path and the cabin came back into sight, Shirley realized that it already felt like she'd been coming here for years.

It took just one visit to the cabin, and Shirley and Jack had fallen in love with it. In 1951, their daughter Annie was born, and they badly wanted to take her up north and show her the tadpoles in the ditches and the minnows in the shallow parts of the river. As soon as they were able, they began making plans to spend as many weekends up north as they could.

It became a regular event, those quick summer visits to the cabin. Jack,

Shirley, Johnny and Annie spent many long weekends there, fishing from the small aluminum boat that was Cliff Hale's, digging in the soft sand by the river, swimming in the gentle current of the Au Sable, and racing up the huge, steep forested hill behind the dam to explore in the woods.

On a typical cabin weekend, Shirley would run to the grocery store and stock up on the basic essentials: bread, milk, cereal, snacks, soda, hot dogs. By early evening, she'd have everything ready and they'd quickly load it all up in the station wagon when Jack got home from work. Jack drove, and Shirley spent much of the ninety minute drive turned, facing the middle seat, cooing and coddling the little ones. They'd arrive at dusk, slowly pulling down the bumpy road that led to the cabin. They could see deer leaping out of site, into the woods behind the cabin as the rumbling car approached. It wasn't long before Shirley and Jack were spending weeks instead of weekends up there; at some point they began to want more time in the quiet, peaceful rooms of the cabin, deep in the woods, doing nothing.

Those days the Causgroves spent at the cabin were true vacation days; Jack often relaxed in the deep old rocking chair that had once belonged to his father-in-law, puffing on his pipe and creaking back and forth. Shirley got the kids up in the morning, helped them down from the top bunk, and after breakfast, got them in their bathing suits. Off the foursome would walk in the early morning sun of a hot July day; it was a quick five minute walk to the gently sloping sandy bank and the Au Sable River, stubbing toes and chasing hopping frogs and dragonflies. They spent their mornings at the river, skipping stones and splashing tiny children's feet in the clear water. Shirley would pull her dark, short hair up and wade in the warm water, guiding the kids along as they took their first swimming lessons. Jack would sometimes teach the kids to search for tadpoles in the creeks; other times he watched from the shore, sitting cross-legged in the sand and letting the sun warm him through. The days were slow and easy, which was what he loved.

Lunch back at the cool cabin was always welcome; off came the swimming trunks and little piles of sand began to dot the cabin floor. After sandwiches or sloppy Joes, the afternoons would wind down in a carefree way with naps, reading, and coloring. Dusk and the slightly cooler breezes always brought the sleepy family to life again. As soon as the sun set and the early crickets started chirping, Jack and Shirley would herd the kids back into the car, and they'd head off for a drive down the back road.

The back road was carved out by the Consumer Powers energy company to give necessary access to their string of power lines; visitors to the cabin use the miles of road to easily explore the otherwise impenetrable woods. This deeply rutted road twists and turns its way deep into the Huron Forest, so narrow at times that trees and branches often threaten to take off a weak antenna or side car mirror; you can't worry about your car's paint job on that road. It leads those who follow it to stunning vistas high above the Au Sable, then plunges back into the dark, dense forest and continues snaking through the trees.

The back road held the promise of adventure every night for the young Causgrove family. Dusk was the time that the deer would come out to feed; the forest back then was overflowing with them. It was thrilling for Johnny and Annie to spot the brown deer, with their soft eyes and nervous twitching ears, who watched them with alert curiosity as the car lurched slowly through their grazing ground. Shirley and Jack never got tired of watching the graceful animals at their routine feeding. Sometimes the animals would simply watch the invading humans; the more fearful ones would leap away with a flick of a tail to the security of the inner forest.

The back road did eventually come to an end, and at the turnaround, Jack would maneuver a tricky three-point turn, avoiding the tree stumps created by beavers and huge ruts in the ground. On the drive back to the cabin, evening would already be several shades darker, with just a touch of dim smoky-orange light burning in the sky above the trees. Out would come the flashlights; the kids would nearly fall out of the car windows in excitement as they shone the penetrating beams into the grassy fields and forest edges to catch the glint of deer eyes in the darkness. Often the children would let out a shriek, sending any remaining deer leaping in perfect gracefulness into the woods and quickly out of sight.

A feeling of quiet contentment would fill the dusty station wagon as it exited the gritty potholed back road and lurched back on to the solid dirt of Cooke Dam Road; another successful deer adventure for the family memory books. Two minutes later back at the cabin and the kids would be shouting about what was for dinner and dessert.

Jack and Shirley often invited the weathered Cooke Dam operators to dinner on those summer weekends up north. The large, green oval wooden table in the cabin kitchen was built strong and sturdy, able to hold many elbows and with room for broad shoulders; the matching chairs could support any hungry guests welcomed to the table. For her family and their up north friends, Shirley set out a feast of thick fire-grilled steaks, steaming potatoes and crisp fresh vegetables. The beer was passed round and laughter and tall tales flew around the table. The old green chairs would creak as the men leaned forward for seconds; would scrape on the rough floor as they pushed back their chairs to relax, hearts and stomachs full. If anyone had room, and most people did, Shirley served pieces of homemade apple pie dotted with butter and cinnamon on mismatched dessert plates.

The laughter would continue long after nighttime settled in and took over. The stars had been out for hours before the men even thought about leaving. They hated to leave; dinner and warmth like this was a rare and treasured diversion from the often solitary life of a dam operator on the Au Sable. The kids would start to nod off and the guests knew it was time to leave. Heartfelt thanks were passed around and the men would disappear into their cars and chug off back to the dam. Shirley would put off doing the dishes to sit on the huge couch, a child on either side of her, and read to the sleepy kids by the light of a few dim candles. Then, in their soft pajamas, the kids would be tucked into bed in the top bunk, asleep by the time Shirley would tiptoe out to the kitchen.

In 1959, after a tragically short marriage, Shirley's husband Jack passed away from liver cancer. At thirty-five, Shirley was still a young woman, but she never remarried; Jack had been the love of her life.

Shortly after Jack passed away, Cliff and Helen Hale bought the Thomas' half of the cabin; after fourteen years of hunting camaraderie, Jack Thomas claimed there were not enough deer in the forest anymore to keep him interested. The cabin now belonged exclusively to the Hales. Cliff and Helen continued to make the drive up north every year for hunting season, bringing along with them a very old and slower-moving Cookie, the little spotted dog. Shirley was now a young single mother of two, who still loved the cabin and wanted to make the drive up there as often as possible. She found it easier and more enjoyable to go up with her mama and daddy, so she often drove along with them for hunting season.

****

Packing for the early winter weather was vastly different than packing for a hot hazy July weekend, like Shirley had been used to doing with Jack. It was thick flannel shirts instead of bathing suits, ear muffs instead of flip-flops, and warm lined leather gloves instead of cut-off shorts.

The new family group of Cliff, Helen, Shirley, Johnny, Annie and Cookie made for a tightly packed car as they drove up north every second week in November. They went up for the hunting, then stayed through

Thanksgiving, which was an especially warm and special time at the cabin. Frequently there would be a fresh, glinting snowfall on the ground, making the dark blond wood of the cabin shine clean and crisp. The little stove inside would warm up the cold floor boards, recently covered with tile (an anniversary gift for Cliff and Helen), giving the inside a finished look. The frozen pump had to be primed immediately upon arrival, and the little stove turned on to heat up the water in pots.

Sometimes the whole family would drive into town for the annual Oscoda bingo game; the grand prize was a huge turkey for the dinner table. Win or lose at the bingo game, Shirley and Helen served a huge, piping hot Thanksgiving dinner every year up at the cabin, with varying numbers of friends and family gathered round the big green oval table with the green and white checked tablecloth. As the plates were passed around for mashed potatoes or squash, it might be noticed that none of the plates matched; some were round, some were square. Guests might also notice that none of the silverware matched, nor did more than two chairs placed around the table. Shirley knew it, and she knew that's what she and her whole family loved so much about their cabin.

A year had passed since Jack died; Shirley found herself spending more time with her mother and father and growing closer to them than she ever had been. She found comfort with these two loving parents, as she struggled to carry on after the death of her husband. They cared for her and supported her when she needed it the most.

That November as they were making bustling plans for their annual trip into the woods and to their cabin, Cliff quietly made the observation to his oldest daughter that this might be Cookie's last trip up north. On the drive up, Shirley turned around to look at the beloved family dog, curled up on an old sweatshirt in the backseat of their car, between the two kids. She had indeed grown very old and slow over the past months; every move had become difficult and troublesome. They all helped her as much as they could, picking her up and into the car and carrying her on walks whenever necessary. They knew that the time was soon coming when they would miss their Cookie nosing her way in and out of the screened doors of the cabin, racing around in the woods and sleeping on a corner of the couch at night.

Animals have a sense of when they are going to die. We humans who love them can only watch with teary eyes, and give our beloved pets whatever help we can during their last days as our companions. Our pets do know what they're doing; they go when they've said their good-byes and are ready.

The Hales arrived late afternoon that November. Shirley carried Cookie inside when they got there; Helen lit the stove and Cliff primed the pump. Cookie stood in the middle of the cabin, observing all through dim eyes. She turned and went slowly to the front door, asking in her quiet way to go outside. Cliff let her out, and set her gently down in the soft springy ground under the evergreen trees. She ambled off, nose to the ground. Cliff came inside and helped Helen and Shirley finish unpacking food, clothes, and books. The minutes passed.

Routinely Helen went outside and called to Cookie, and listened for the sound of the leaves crackling, or her collar jingling to signal that the little dog had heard and was heading back. An hour passed and Helen, straining to hear anything, began to worry. She took a few steps and called again, louder and more insistent; still only the quiet, sweet hush of twilight. Helen took a step off the cabin step and called quickly to Cliff and Shirley. Together they walked around the side of the cabin and into the woods directly in back. There they found their little Cookie. She had chosen her time, and place.

Shirley was glad she had been there for her parents that November. That night, with eyes red from crying, this family who had grown so close buried their little wire-haired terrier Cookie in the woods in back of the cabin. After all, it was the place she had chosen.

****

In 2004, about two dozen of Cliff and Helen's offspring, old and young, celebrated Shirley Causgrove's 80th birthday. Laughing family members gathered around the big country table in the sunny dining room on Aunt Janie's twenty acre farm in western Michigan. We cheered Aunt Shirley on to blow out all the candles on her huge cake, decorated with a girl in a bikini on a beach. Rounding out the party of birthday well-wishers outside were two cart ponies, thirty feisty chickens, one peacock, several cats, and three dogs. What was ostensibly a yearly family reunion was secretly a surprise birthday party for Aunt Shirley, still beautiful with gray hair, a youthful face and a quick smile.

Today she is the head of all cabin activities. Aunt Shirley keeps the calendar up to date so that no two parties end up at the cabin front door, cars jam-packed with radios, fishing rods, and coolers, at the same time.

Aunt Shirley is the one who knows how to shimmy the pump turn-screw off at the end of the cabin season. She is the one who can always get the fussy little stove started, and knows how to drain the pipes at the end of October. She and her daughter Annie keep the cabin mouse and bat-free, so the rest of us don't have to even think about things like that. She also knows how to find reliable handymen in town to fix things when they sag, and who to call when the oil tank outside gets low.

I often refer to Aunt Shirley as the Keeper of the Cabin, because that's just what she does, and what she has done for the past thirty-plus years. The cabin is full of old pictures she has put up, knick-knacks she has placed on side tables, and potholders she has bought from the downtown store. When there is any important (or even non-important) question about anything concerning the cabin, "Ask Aunt Shirley" is what we all say first. More than anything she has brought the warmth of the cabin into all of our lives by her generous, helpful ways, and with her desire to pass on a priceless family tradition to the next generation of stone-skippers and tadpole catchers.

Aunt Shirley at the cabin

Patricia Hale

Patricia Hale

1926 was the year of the first phone call between New York and London; NBC first came into existence; <u>Winnie the Pooh</u> was written; and on March 7, Cliff and Helen welcomed their second daughter Patricia Ann into their lives. These loving parents carried another second-hand crib into the upstairs bedrooms; Pat joined Shirley in the growing Hale nursery on South Chilson Street. The rooms upstairs with the creaking wooden floorboards were full of gingham, lace, knitted blankets, flowered wallpaper, and homemade stuffed animals that Helen had made.

Cliff took a little time off from the hardware store when Pat was born but as manager, he couldn't take much. That spring turned quickly into summer and on the weekends, Helen would sit outside with the two little girls, bouncing them on her knees while Cliff, kneeling, tended to his garden in the back yard; as the afternoon heated up, he'd roll up his sleeves, weeding and pruning. Helen would put the girls in bed for a nap and come back outside in the sun with Clifford, running inside every now and then to check on dinner which would be simmering on the stove by late afternoon.

Cliff and Helen loved being parents. They adored their daughters and gave them as much as they could afford. The family went to quiet neighborhood parks, fed the birds, bought bicycles at local flea markets. They didn't go out to eat much; Helen was a good cook and there was always more food than they needed. They went to church every Sunday, walking if the weather was nice.

Pat and older sister Shirley naturally grew into best friends. They were close enough in age that they almost always had the same interests, whether it was dolls, clothes, horses, or books. The two girls grew up and through grade school and high school were almost inseparable; Pat felt very alone when Shirley married and moved out of the house. Pat kept in touch with her older sister even as friends, boyfriends, and a career kept her life full.

Shirley and Pat Hale

By the time the Hales and Thomas's started talking in earnest about building a deer hunting cabin, Pat had grown into a beautiful young woman of 20 with sandy blond hair, blue eyes, and Lauren Bacall cheekbones. She had graduated from Bay City High School and decided she wanted to study to be a nurse. She took a few belongings and moved away from her pale green house on the quiet street to attend nursing school in Saginaw; Pat was away during all the talk at home about building a cabin in the woods up north. Whenever she had a free weekend from school, she made the drive home to unwind and visit with her family, relaxing in the rocking chairs on the front porch as evening came, sipping lemonade and catching up. On one of the warm summer nights at home, her daddy told Pat about the cabin he was building; Pat's career and school were at the forefront of her life and the cabin didn't hold her interest for too long.

It was on one of those quiet summer weekends when Pat was visiting that her mother and father convinced her to make the drive up north to see the beginnings of the cabin, which by then had a floor and a few partial walls. Pat agreed, and early the next morning the Hales and the Thomas's formed a two-car caravan as they headed up to the Huron Forest.

Their little party was made up of Cliff and Helen, Shirley, Pat and Cookie; Jack, Agnes, and six year old Judy Thomas. To Cliff and Jack, this trip was becoming routine; they had been driving up north every weekend to check on the progress of their dream cabin, and to pitch in and help. The wives had been going too, to be with their families and enjoy the time spent away from the kitchen and laundry.

On the drive up that morning, Pat tried not to think about nursing school, but she had tests coming up, she had a date next weekend, she had books to buy; school occupied her mind that day. She chatted with Judy absentmindedly, vaguely watching the Midwest farmland gradually turn into dense pine forests through the car window. Traffic thinned and soon they were winding their way on a dirt road along the serene, scenic Au Sable River; suddenly they slowed and turned, bumping along a grassy road heading straight into the woods.

The cars jolted to a stop in front of a chaotic construction scene: the foundation of the small cabin, sawdust, chopped trees, building materials, and an old trailer where Uncle Bill was living that summer. Bill's little Jack Russell Terriers came running out of the woods, barking at the two families as they pushed the creaking car doors open and stepped out into the fresh air.

Pat got out and looked around her, a newcomer to the scene. For the first time that day, all thoughts of school vanished. She slowly picked her way through the piles of wood and tools to stand on the floor of her father's cabin. Breathing deeply, she took it all in. She looked around her at the woods, the trees swaying gently in the breeze on that summer afternoon. The air was fresh and clean, the forest quiet, the sun warm, the sky blue. Her feet were already covered in sawdust as she gingerly stepped around pieces of lumber to all four corners of the cabin.

The men stood in a group apart, discussing the progress, and Cliff pointed out what he wanted done differently. Bill was sweating already from the work he'd done that morning, and was more than happy to take a break; he settled himself onto a log half listening to Cliff. Pat was excited, and in an instant knew she wanted to be a part of this, man's deer hunting cabin or not. She hopped off the foundation and interrupted her father to tell him she really liked it here. Smiling, Cliff excused himself and he and Pat walked off together down the bumpy road and towards the river.

This was Pat's first visit to the banks of the Au Sable, the first time she watched the fish jump and dug her toes in the warm sand. She and her daddy sat in the sun and just watched the river, talking only occasionally.

Time spent in that way passes too quickly; they returned to the cabin a few hours later. Pat loved her first taste of the river, walking on the sandy shore barefoot and exploring the gently rising dunes. Any thoughts of school were a definite distraction up here in the woods. Dusk settled in on Pat's first night up north. Dam operator Art Clement and his wife welcomed the Hales and the Thomas's into their home for the night, as they did whenever the families were up north and needed a place to stay. Emma Clement laid out a beautiful dinner for their guests, friends and family breaking up into smaller groups around small tables. As they ate dinner they watched the sun slowly set over the river through the huge picture windows. The laughing and talking continued late into the night.

****

After that first visit up north, Pat went up with her mother and father whenever she could; she could not wait for the cabin to be finished. Her love affair with the forest, the cabin and the river had begun.

By late August, the cabin had four walls, two doors, eleven windows, two bedrooms and two bunk beds; the only thing missing was the roof. On one weekend visit, the weather was so mild that Pat and Shirley, after much begging, were allowed to spend the night in the roofless cabin, under the stars. Joined by their two younger sisters, Pat and Shirley whispered late into the night, listening to the rustlings of the deer and the raccoons in the forest around them. Soon the owls took over and then finally, silence. From that first night on, the little cabin had a place in Pat's heart.

After that, she was hooked. A routine formed; the men would spend the weekends up north hammering, sawing, measuring, while the women took walks and helped out where they could. Weather permitting, at night after dinner, Pat, Shirley and sometimes Judy would spend the night in the cabin without a roof. Summers don't last long enough in Michigan's north and it wasn't long before those beautiful, endless August days and nights dwindled away.

That first peaceful summer of forest walks and mysterious, warm nights under the stars came to an end when the cool winds of October began to whip through the Huron woods. Pat returned to school and stopped coming home as often; her nursing career again took over and instead of open-air cabins and the hot sun along the river, she became wrapped up in dorm rooms, classes, and girlfriend gossip.

Cliff and Jack first started using the cabin that November for hunting, taking their rifles, boots, and warm woolen coats as they loaded up the car. The wives followed along a day or two later, enjoying each other's company as they kept the cabin warm and cozy, fixing lunches and dinners for their returning husbands.

The debut of the hunting cabin that year was a huge success. The two men got to be out in the huge, nearly empty expanse of northern woods, rifles slung across their shoulders, their breath coming out in puffs as they crouched for hours in their hides. The wives' friendship deepened as they sat in the little warm cabin, knitting, cooking, and telling each other stories of their children. These two women, devoted as they were to Cliff and Jack, daily shared a very private joke at their husbands' expense; the wives would often laugh at how many deer they would see through the frosty cabin windows, picking their way through the forest, and the men would come home at night complaining that they hadn't seen any deer yet again that day.

****

Four years passed since Pat spent her first night up north at the cabin. She had graduated from nursing school and got her first job at Saginaw General Hospital as a clinical instructor. She met and fell in love with a handsome, young, former gymnast turned insurance salesman named Bill Ahrens; the two of them were married in October of 1950.

Pat and Bill were a young couple, just starting out. They had dreams of buying a house and starting a family; their income, even combined, was modest. Their wedding was quiet and simple; thoughts of long, glamorous, exotic honeymoons had drifted in and out of their pre-wedding plans. In the end, Pat had the very practical idea of spending their honeymoon up north at her parents' hunting cabin.

This idea seemed anything but romantic to Pat and Bill. The young couple had been browsing through glossy travel brochures and reading about Hawaii, Florida, the Carolinas; the cabin idea seemed to fall far short. But in the end, that's what they chose; most of their money had been spent on their wedding. They decided to make the best of it and began making plans for their up north honeymoon. As they packed their old station wagon full of both warm and cold weather clothes, books and magazines, beer and soda, Pat and Bill giggled and grinned at each other over the hood of their car; even though they were just going up north, they were excited. Pat hoped the cabin could deliver a week of romantic memories for her and her new husband.

All her concerns faded as they bounced down the little grassy lane, through the old crooked wooden gate and straight up to the cabin front door. The cabin had been closed since the last hunting trip, many months ago. The curtains were drawn shut, doors locked, pump a little rusty. Bill struggled a bit with the lock, and the two of them finally stepped inside a very cold, dark, quiet cabin. Pat fumbled around in the old cupboard next to the front door for stashed candles and long wooden matches; she got a few of those lit and placed them around the little room as her confidence began to grow. She smiled at Bill in the late afternoon and began to open the curtains and fluff up the pillows on the old couch and chairs; light began to stream in. They unloaded their car and got the oil heater going with foot-long wooden matches and a little coaxing.

They picked out what they wanted for dinner and Bill got a fire going outside. Pat glanced at her husband, very much in love. This was their first night together as a married couple. Pat realized she was out in the middle of the woods, in a cozy, warm cabin with a full ice box; no one else was around except the man she loved. She knew then they had chosen the only perfect spot for their honeymoon.

The young couple spent the next 6 days holding hands, taking lazy walks through the woods, dipping their feet in the cooling river and catching a glimpse of deer and wild turkey. Except when they drove into town, they didn't see another soul; in the forest, it seemed like they were the only two people in the universe. Time seemed to be standing still for them.

They enjoyed every minute of their honeymoon. Indian summer was in full swing that week; they were thrilled when each day turned out warm and sunny, rare for upper Michigan in October. Each morning Pat would make a big pot of strong, black coffee; they would snuggle closely and make their plans. During the day they would slowly wander through the woods or along the water for hours, finding old paths or making new ones; they slept in, read books, played cards, and waded in the river. Once or twice they drove into town, to watch a movie at the tiny little .25 theater, or to get groceries. At night they would sit side by side on the big couch as the sun went down, reading by the low light of short squat candles or playing cards, and listening to the crickets outside. Nighttime at the cabin was peaceful and quiet, with a hush settling and closing in.

Pat and Bill's honeymoon up north transformed the cabin into more than just a deer hunter's cabin. Suddenly, all of the Hales had a place to escape to, a place to take the kids to, a vacation spot, a romantic getaway; the possibilities were endless.

A year after their romantic honeymoon at the cabin, Pat gave birth to their first son Michael, in 1951. This young family started a tradition of going up to the cabin each summer in June, and staying for two weeks. Seven years later, Pat and Bill had brought Vickie, Julie, and Steve into the world; the Ahrens' summers up at the cabin had become a yearly event. Parents and kids alike looked forward to those June visits of fresh air and bonfires, sand and sun. They started to make their summer cabin plans as soon as the Christmas season was over.

Mike, Bill and Pat Ahrens

****

Before the days of total electronic pastimes and digital entertainment, kids spent their time outdoors, climbing trees, making forts, playing hide and seek. The cabin was the ultimate fantasy land for this kind of old-fashioned kid fun. The Thomas's kids loved it up there; Shirley and Jack and their kids loved it up there; Pat and Bill's kids could not wait to pack up the car every summer and get up north, where the adventures waited.

In the woods, animal holes, wasps' nests, frogs, wildflowers and swamps begged to be discovered. Bill was an excellent swimmer and taught all of the kids how to swim in the river; Pat would sit on the shore keeping an eye on her four growing children. Often they walked to Cooke Dam and then across, racing up the steep forested hill behind the dam to unexplored territory. The kids usually found their way across the bluff to a huge dune, that today we still call Ahrens' dune, and tumble all the way down. At the bottom they'd run in the river in their shorts to cool off.

The family's river fun was augmented when Bill donated an old boat motor to the cabin; they hooked it up to Cliff's aluminum fishing boat. After they dragged it down to the river, they would spend hours zipping up and down the Au Sable, peering into the clear depths below or sometimes actually fishing over the side.

In the late afternoons, the family would sometimes pile into the car in their sandy bathing suits and head into town, all the windows rolled down, for ice cream or window shopping at the boutiques and dime stores. There was a beautiful park in Tawas on Lake Huron where the kids could swing and see-saw, or chase the squawking seagulls in the waves along the shore;

Pat and Bill would watch quietly, holding hands and soaking up the last rays of a lazy summer afternoon. Nighttime at the cabin brought out the kindling and the hot dogs, marshmallows and chocolate. The kids had hollowed out a fire pit and learned how to build a roaring fire; they found their favorite roasting sticks and before long all had sticky fingers from the soot and the simmering, gooey marshmallows. Each day ended the same: two exhausted but happy parents and four kids who fell asleep in the big bunk beds the minute their heads hit their pillows.

Ahrens' and Berkemeiers: Crickie, Matthew, Don, Jennifer, Julie, Steve, Pat, Mike

These memorable summers up at the cabin continued even as the four Ahrens children grew up into young adults. All the kids were active, athletic and outgoing, and they all joined multiple sports teams and other activities in high school. One year however, the football and cheerleading schedules suddenly seemed to take over Pat's life and as she started to plan for the summer up north, she came to the realization that they just couldn't go up that year; the kids were too busy with their teams, choirs, and plays. Sadly, Pat resolved to make up for it next year; next summer came and went and the Ahrens' had to skip the summer up at the cabin again.

It was sometime in the early '70s that the Ahrens' stopped going up north to the cabin in the summer; after that, they never went up to the cabin again as a family. The kids had years of memories though; none of them would forget those days of skipping stones in the river and roasting s'mores over an open fire. Pat had her memories too, and often during football games, cheerleading competitions, band recitals and graduations her mind would wander back and see those same children racing up and down the big dunes up north, and curling up next to her on the huge couch at night in the little cabin.

As Pat's children grew up, the years seemed to race by. One by one, they graduated high school and then moved on, either to college or permanent, full-time jobs that kept them away from home. Not used to having empty time on her hands, Pat went back to work part-time to fill her days. She and Bill settled into a predictable existence of scrapbooks, TV dinners, evening sitcoms, and after- dinner drinks.

Pat's life had changed; it was now so different from the happy, fulfilling days of raising her children, taking them up north every year for the hot, fun summers at the cabin. Truthfully, she rarely thought of the cabin anymore as she sank into her new role of a mom whose kids had all grown up and moved away. Admittedly, she lost some of that purpose in life that she once had, lost the exuberant joy of youth and the adventure of raising four lovely children. Without realizing it, she had also drifted apart from her sister Shirley, the person who had been her best friend for much of her life. Daily life consisted of working part-time, hoping to get a phone call from one of her kids, cleaning the house and cooking simple meals for her and Bill to share while watching game shows in their favorite easy chairs at night. The love and excitement she had for the forest and the cabin was lost for the time being. She was nothing like the young, vibrant girl who had stood on the foundation of the cabin in its infancy, and walked over to her father to tell him how much she loved it up north. Time had taken a toll on Pat, and the thought of going up north again just seemed too difficult, so she put it out of her mind.

The years went by and the cabin now stood empty for much of the summer, the curtains closed, the doors and windows locked, the antique dressers collecting dust. Seasons came and went; Pat's memory of four kids racing up the dune, building sandcastles, and hunting for frogs in the woods faded. Vague echoes of laughter in the woods from her children were all that was left of Pat's cherished vacations up north with her family. For Pat, life trudged on.

She is not sure what happened, but something made Pat push herself up out of her recliner one morning and make a determined decision that she needed change in her life. Perhaps it was one too many talk shows watched, one too many TV dinners eaten. On New Year's Day in 1979, Pat called Shirley, who she rarely spoke to anymore, except on holidays or birthdays. Shirley had to sit down as she listened to Pat; the phone call had caught her by complete surprise. Shirley needed to make sure she was hearing it correctly.

"Shirley, would you like to go up north to the cabin with me this summer in June?"

It had taken Pat several weeks to work up the courage to call her sister and make the suggestion. Although it seemed that her memories had been lost, Pat had never really forgotten the joy she felt in being up north, walking through the woods or cooking over the old stove at the cabin. She needed some up north fresh air and rustling of leaves at that time in her life. The love between the two sisters had not faded, and of course Shirley agreed to meet her younger sister up north that summer. Pat put down the phone and looked around her faded living room, and wondered how she would keep herself occupied until she could drive up north and once again open up the curtains in the cabin to let the sunlight in.

June finally did arrive, and Pat had dug through closets and drawers to find her old cabin things. She dusted off the cooler, found her fishing rod, and wiped the binoculars clean. Giving Bill a few last minute cooking instructions, she called to their dog Mason, who eagerly jumped into the front seat with Pat as she backed down their driveway and turned the car north.

Shirley, having the shorter drive, had arrived at the cabin first, and had coffee brewing and pastries out on the big oval kitchen table, waiting for her sister. Pat turned down the dirt road and drove through the old white gate, getting her first glimpse of the little log cabin in too many years. She was overcome with nostalgia and tears welled up in her eyes; she pulled up to the cabin crying. Shirley came outside to help Pat unload the car, and was greeted by a panting Mason, who immediately raced around the cabin and into the woods. Wiping the tears from her eyes, Pat and Shirley met on the unkempt front lawn of the cabin and hugged each other. "It's good to see you, Shirley", Pat said as the two embraced. These two sisters who hadn't seen each other in years, now walked into the cabin together, to the same rooms where they had once slept side by side, under the stars, almost thirty years ago. Together they unloaded the car, and then sat down at the creaking oval kitchen table and sipped coffee, while the warm Huron breezes blew in the open windows. They had years of catching up to do.

Pat and Shirley spent two weeks up north that June, getting to know each other, and the cabin, all over again. They walked the same familiar paths in the woods, and found some new ones too. They barbequed dinner down by the river, and took lawn chairs to watch the bright orange sunsets over the far banks. At the end of the two weeks, they made a promise to each other to come up again next June for two weeks. And true to their promise, these two sisters again met on the front lawn of the cabin that following June. The June vacations became a new tradition for Shirley and Pat, the cabin no longer standing empty and closed up each warm summer. The joy slowly returned to Pat's life, as she began looking forward each year to the vacation up north with her sister.

As it turned out, Pat had never truly forgotten the happiness of curling up in the big bunk beds at night, driving down the back roads to look for deer, and sitting in the big rocking chair listening to the old, crackling 1940's radio as night closed in.

****

Aunt Pat had finished sharing her cabin memories with me, and we were about to hang up the phone when she suddenly told me to wait; she had remembered something more she wanted to tell me.

After the Thomas' sold their share of the cabin to Cliff Hale, their daughter Judy, who had also fallen in love with the cabin and the river, used to rent a cottage nearby where she would spend a few weekends, and take a summer vacation every year. It had been many years since her family had been a part of Goodnufrus, however the families remained on good terms and she often thought of the Hales and the little cabin that was once a part of her family.

One summer in the late '70s when Judy was up north at her rental, she had a free afternoon and timidly drove down the old road; she wanted to see the old log cabin where she, Pat and Shirley used to spend hunting seasons together over a dozen years ago. The cabin was closed up, so she went next door to Emily's place to see if anyone was home there. (Emily is the older German woman who lived next door, who I remember used to bring us homemade cookies in the mornings in her robe and curlers.) Emily answered Judy's knock and the two embraced, after many years of not seeing each other. Judy wanted to go inside the cabin; her curiosity had gotten her this far and now she didn't want to leave without stepping inside. Emily knew the Hales wouldn't mind, and taking her key the two walked over to the cabin and went in. Judy walked to the middle of the quiet old cabin and looked around; the rugs, kitchen table, photographs, cabinets, deer trophy, rocking chairs, it was all the same. Judy stood there for about a minute then putting her hands over her face, burst into tears as the memories of time spent here came flooding back to her. They had been happy, carefree, loving times with family and friends, and the little cottage she had been renting just wasn't the same. She thanked Emily and hugged her again; taking one last look at the black and white picture of Cliff and Helen tacked to the wall, Judy Thomas turned and left the little cabin for the last time.

****

Just as we did for Shirley in 2004, two years later we celebrated Aunt Pat's 80th birthday in the form of a family reunion at Mike and girlfriend Chris' place on Lake Michigan, near the quaint little town of Pentwater (I highly recommend a visit). We spent the searingly hot July day huffing and puffing up the many stairs built into the dunes to and from Mike and Chris' cabin, lugging mini surfboards, beach balls and arm floaties for the kids. We laughed, we screamed, we were the loudest family on the beach. Sadly, Aunt Pat lost Bill in 1999 from cancer and complications from chemotherapy, but her children, sisters, nieces and nephews were there to wish her well as she cut her cake. That night, we settled in to patio chairs and watched a shimmering orange sunset over the lake that had us all clicking away with our cameras; five tired dogs lay asleep at our feet.

Aunt Pat struggles with numerous health issues, but in spite of that still goes up to the cabin with family as often as she can, in the summer months. She has never again let years go by without making the trip up north, even though at times she has had to have someone drive her, due to her health. She laughs at the old, fading picture of herself on the cabin wall, curled up on her parent's front lawn as a teenager, with horn-rimmed glasses, saddle shoes, and a flipped up bob. We thank Aunt Pat for starting the family tradition of spending our vacations up at the cabin, and of bringing our kids up here to race up and down the dunes, creating childhood memories that last a lifetime.

Pat Hale

Barbara Hale

Bobby Hale

On April 23, 1936, Barbara Mary Hale was born; Cliff and Helen were proud parents again. They named their third daughter Barbara, but friends and family called her Bobby and the nickname stuck. Born 10 years after older sister Pat, she got her own room in the smaller of the two bedrooms upstairs.

Bobby and Shirley were the dark-haired sisters; Bobby had thick brown hair, brown eyes and a clear complexion. She had the same quick laugh as her sisters and mom; she wore hand-me-downs from her sisters but got her own pair of new brown loafers from the shoe store downtown. Helen pulled Bobby's long straight hair back in a ponytail like she did her sisters'. The Hale house was filling up with girls in cotton dresses, pigtails, and old blue jeans.

Bobby was seven years old when her mother and father began staying up late at the dining room table to talk about building a cabin up north. At the time, her parents were already part owners in another cabin in Roscommon, Michigan, 60 miles west of where Cliff and Jack hoped to build their hunting cabin. What the Hales didn't like about the Roscommon cabin was that they were one of four families who were all part owners of that property; Cliff and Jack wanted something they could call their own.

And so the planning started.

The two men wanted a location with lots of deer; that was most important. The families looked around and fell in love with the Huron Forest and the Au Sable River. They pooled what money they could and bought a little piece of land in the dead of the forest, within walking distance of the sandy river.

Their next challenge was to find someone who could build a cabin, and who Cliff and Jack could afford to pay. They approached Bill Campbell, who was Helen's uncle; he worked with his hands building things and seemed to be exactly what the Hales were looking for. To Bobby, "Uncle Bill" was a tiny, thin rickety man who always had a pipe or cigar clenched in one corner of his mouth. His eyes sparkled and would especially light up when he was around kids; they were his joy. His other love was his Jack Russell Terriers Mugsy and Judy, who were always hopping around Bill's feet, begging for attention from the kids. Everyone loved Bill; he was the perfect man for the job. He set himself up in his trailer, with his building supplies and tools, on the little piece of land up north by the river.

Bill did most of the work on the cabin, he and his friend Art Clement. When the Hale family made the trip up north on the weekends, Helen and Cliff brought whatever children could come and they made a family weekend out of it. Bobby used to beg her mother to let her bring a friend up north with them, and Helen usually let her.

Bobby Hale

Once Bobby got her first taste of cool Huron Forest fresh air, she couldn't wait for the weekends when they went up north. Helen would bake homemade apple and blueberry pies, and put them in a cooler along with some soda and beer. She would make soup and chili a day ahead of time and let it simmer on the stove; they would pack that up in stew pots and warm it up on the stove in the Clement's kitchen, where they spent the night on their weekends up north.

On the way up north the station wagon would pull into the local grocery store and Helen would run in, picking up fresh bread, crackers, and milk. To Bobby, the 90 minute drive seemed to take forever in the fading light of a Friday evening. She loved being able to take a friend, which made the time pass more quickly. Older sisters Shirley and Pat were away at school and often not able to go; Bobby and friend, and younger sister Janie would sit in the back seat and play horses or whisper secrets to each other, giggling at their own jokes as the car sped north into the dusk.

It would be nearly dark when the old Hale Ford would jostle and jolt down the bumpy, grassy path to the cabin site. Bill would be done working for the day and, tired and sore, just sitting down for a beer and dinner in his tiny trailer with his dogs. He would be slow to get up but welcomed the family warmly with a smile, enjoying their company. Running up to Bill, Bobby would hug him around his legs and bend down to play with his dogs, laughing at how they licked her face. Cliff and Bill would walk off together, Cliff wanting to know how far Bill had gotten on the cabin; was the floor done yet? The year was 1945 and wood was scarce due to World War II; Bill had been using green, unseasoned lumber and Cliff wanted to know how that was working out. Bobby was oblivious to the whole complex building process, and right away raced off into the woods behind the cabin; Helen would shout at her not go too far and to stay out of the mud.

After visiting with Bill for a while, the Hales and Bill would load back into their car and drive the ¼ mile along the river to Cooke Dam and the Clement house, where Helen would warm up her soup or chili, butter some bread, and grab some ice cold beer and soda pop from the coolers. The families loved these nights with friends, sipping drinks and stretching out after long weeks of work.

Bobby remembers fondly those nights at the Clements; the house overlooked the river and it had an upstairs to explore. The Hales and the Clements sat long around the dinner table, catching up on each other's lives and laughing into the night; the kids, having used up their energy in the woods and full from dinner, would fall fast asleep together on the big couch in the living room.

Saturday morning and the children would be up as soon as the sun poked through the crocheted curtains of the upstairs rooms. They would come clumping down the wide wooden stairs where Helen and Emma Clement would be chatting together and making sausage and pancakes for breakfast. Bobby ate her syrupy pancakes as quickly as possible, fighting the face wash and leisurely departure of her parents; she begged to get back to the cabin site as quickly as possible. She would spend the rest of the day playing hide and seek in the woods, walking down to the river and digging her toes in the warm sand with her father, climbing trees, and playing with Bill's dogs. When Sunday afternoon came and it was time to head back to Bay City, she dragged her feet; she never wanted to leave the forest and the river. Back at her desk at school on Monday, Bobby was already planning the next weekend up north again; she'd bring her bathing suit and climb that new tree she'd found. Those weekends up north in the summer of '45 were the best days any young girl could ask for.

Bill Campbell finished the cabin in one summer; it had a roof, doors that could lock, and a powerful gas-heated pot-bellied stove by hunting season. Cliff and Jack grinned at each other as they packed the station wagon for the first time that November. In went warm mittens, hunting rifles, orange hats and coats, big lace-up lined boots, long johns and extra ammunition. Helen and Agnes Thomas added the woman's touch to the car: homemade muffins, extra scarves, chili, books, candles, and knitting needles. Bobby got to go up with them for the whole season, something she looked forward to all year. The men were happy; they had their hunting cabin and the woods were full of deer. The women got to spend time together, two old friends getting to know one another even better. Bobby spent time playing games with her mother and reading horse books by candlelight at night. That little cabin that Bill built was everything the Hales and Thomas's had hoped it would be.

For the first few years of its existence, the Hale cabin was opened up and used only in November for deer hunting season; it seemed to have no other purpose. The rest of the year, through beautiful breezy summers and crisp falls, the curtains remained pulled across the windows and the doors locked.

With young children of their own now, Bobby's older sisters Shirley and Pat started to make the trip up north with their families during the hot, lazy days of summer, swimming in the river and canoeing the graceful, scenic bends of the Au Sable. They started a vacation tradition in the Hale family, and the cabin came to life with the extra use, being opened up every other weekend. Screens were put on the windows to let in the warm summer breezes, an old aluminum boat was bought, fishing poles were found, and a fire pit was built outside. Bobby got caught up in the summer excitement and was soon pleading with her mom and dad to take her and sometimes a friend up north for those hot weekends. It wasn't long before Cliff, Helen, and Bobby were packing up the car with warm weather cabin supplies and making the familiar drive up north starting in June.

From the time she was thirteen years old, Bobby spent as many summer weekends up north as she could. She got to know the 90 minute drive on the highways and county dirt roads by heart. She always had a new book, toy or bathing suit packed in her overnight bag next to her. She often peeked at the homemade cake her mom had made, sitting at her feet in the cooler.

One of Cliff's favorite parts of going up north was to let an eager Cookie out of the car as soon as the family turned off Cooke Dam Road and on to Jennie Street. Their little dog would race after the car as it made the final bumpy drive towards the unkempt lawn of the cabin. Bobby would be the second one out of the car when it came to a halt at the front door in the twilight of a Friday night, running up the concrete steps and rattling the metal handle of the dark green screen door, hopping up and down waiting for her dad to come up behind her with the key. The cabin was always chilly when they first walked inside; it warmed up quickly when the windows were open and the balmy air would begin to slowly blow through the kitchen and living room. Bobby would run into one of the bedrooms and throw her bag on the upper bunk. She loved sleeping on the upper bunks; up high and away from everyone else, she had her privacy. Even better, she had to climb up a narrow, dark crooked ladder to get there. The birdseye view from the lofty top bunk was the other reason she always wanted to sleep there.

Saturdays up north were wide open expanses waiting to be filled. Helen cooked breakfast and dinners using kerosene, and Bobby and younger sister Janie would each pick a big green chair and eat pancakes and sausage at the big oval table in a hurry, then sit near the windows in the creaky kitchen chairs and read comic books by the morning light. The birds would flit and chirp right outside the windows, and the warm summer breezes were already drifting through the cabin. Finally their mom and dad would be ready and off they would walk, down the bumpy cabin road to the dirt road that led to the river. The road was too rough to walk barefoot, but as soon as they got to the river, Bobby's sandals would come off and she'd race down to the river's edge, slipping up to her knees in the warm river water. The kids would tear off their beach cover-ups and swim for hours, Bobby diving to the bottom and practicing back and front somersaults. She liked to see how long she could hold her breath and how far out into the river she could swim. Helen always had a sun-warmed towel waiting for her when she came dripping and sandy out of the water.

Lunch was something quick, maybe hot dogs and homemade lemonade back at the cabin, and then the family would head out again, in the other direction this time, towards Cooke Dam. Sometimes they would drop in on the Clements and visit with them for a while, Bobby always anxious to be back outside. After leaving the Clements, they would cross the river by walking across the dam and hike up the big, steep forested hill beyond that took them to a heady cliff overlooking the river and the soft dunes. In those days, hidden in the woods at the top of the cliff there were several tiny cottages and a little wooden, one-room family store called The Bissonette Resort, where the Hales would get ice cream and pop; they would sit outside at an old picnic table and lick their cones in the afternoon sun. When the adults were rested, they'd all come tumbling back down the hill and slowly make their way back to the cabin for a hot, homemade dinner and some apple pie.

If they had enough energy after dinner, Cliff and Helen would sit around candles as the forest outside got dark and read their latest favorite books; Bobby would pull out her newest comic book or horse adventure story. The night air got a little cool and the crickets would start chirping. One by one, heads nodding, the Hales drifted off to the big soft bunk beds, which creaked as they rolled in. Half asleep and in the dark, Bobby would feel her way up the narrow ladder to her top bunk, blowing out the candle that was hanging in a sconce on the bedroom wall. Her head would hit the pillow and Bobby was asleep, sandy and with untidy pigtails.

Sundays were just as lazy as Saturdays up north. Helen would be up first, cooking bacon and eggs in her bathrobe and slippers. Smelling the breakfast sizzling, Bobby would stumble out into the kitchen rubbing her eyes and give her mom and dad hugs. She'd dig out a deck of cards from the old wooden chest of drawers and play a game of solitaire, sipping on orange juice and sleepily waiting for breakfast. The family would eat together and clean up the kitchen. Bobby would ruffle into her overnight bag and pull out a pair of shorts and a t-shirt; always the first one ready, she had to sit and wait for her mom and dad, and try to be patient.

One of the things Cliff liked to do on Sundays was, when they were old enough, teach his girls how to shoot a rifle. He would pace off down the outhouse path and put some rusty beer cans on a stump or rock. Bobby would sit or stand on the front porch steps and blast away at the cans, getting better and better with each try, the shots ringing out in the morning forest stillness. Her dad showed her how to load the gun and how to handle it safely. Bobby loved to practice, loved the feel of the smooth rifle in her hands and by the time she was a teenager, she had good aim and was a decent shot.

Cliff also loved to take Bobby and her younger sister deep into the woods with nothing but a compass, and show them all the different plants and trees, swamps, animal tracks, homes and nests. The three of them would walk for hours in the dense forest, discovering nature together and wondering, would they be able to find their way home in time for Helen's lunch? They always found their way back, and after lunch they'd all head off back to the river for more swimming or tanning on the warm sand. Late afternoon back at the cabin and Helen would begin to clean up, prodding Bobby to gather her cards, comic books, and tennis shoes into her bag and help load the car. The Hales would pull the curtains across the windows, tidy up one last time, lock the doors and say good-bye to the cabin until the next lazy weekend they could make the drive and open everything back up again.

****

In 1953 Cliff finally grew tired of lighting candles, using an ice box instead of a refrigerator, and cooking with a kerosene stove when they were up north; Cliff wanted electricity in his cabin.   He contacted the electric company, and was told that until a majority of cabin owners in the area also wanted the service, he could keep reading by candlelight. Undaunted, Cliff went on foot and by car to the residents who lived or had cabins in the area, asking them to sign a petition to bring electricity to their part of the Huron Forest. After months of soliciting signatures, and having Bobby type letters on their old typewriter, he finally succeeded with the electric company and they brought their towers and lines into Goodnufrus and the surrounding other cabins.

The Hales were thrilled with the new power; they no longer had to worry about candles, and they bought an old refrigerator and a used stove. They could read without straining their eyes at night, and not worry about tripping over things in the dark. The family looked forward to their summer weekend trips up north even more. Bobby loved the old candleholders, the lanterns, and the sconces, but like everyone else soon got accustomed to the newfound luxuries of electricity. The last two years before Bobby graduated high school, she got to enjoy the new power at the cabin when they'd visit; it only added to the fun of being up north. They added an old wooden radio to the cabin, which they set on the antique buffet in the living room; they'd listen to the crackly radio station at night while reading by the dim lights. Helen could store her food longer, and make the breakfasts quicker. Bobby liked to read in bed at night, which she could now do. The new electricity made it that much harder to leave the cabin after a summer weekend.

Those summer days up north continued for Bobby as she grew up. Often the family would take friends with them, Bobby staying up later

74

as she got older, sitting around the table playing euchre with the adults till after midnight. Even through her late teens, Bobby looked forward to going up north as often as she could. No matter her age, the trips up north were both an adventure and an escape that she treasured.

****

Years passed and Bobby graduated high school. She began dating and hanging out with her girlfriends; her mind turned towards her future. She followed in the footsteps of her older sister Pat and chose a career in nursing. With that decision came Junior College and then nursing school; Bobby had to trade her outdoor weekends up north for daunting nursing textbooks, dormitories, and cafeteria food. She missed the cabin, but she was moving on to a different phase in her life; she was growing up.   No matter how immersed she became in her academic life however, Bobby always knew as she set her alarm for the early shift at the hospital or crammed at night for a test the next day, that she would be back at her cabin one day, enjoying the forest breezes and the big sandy river that were forever a part of her life.

Bobby Hale started her nursing career with Junior College in 1955. She worked hard and was a good student.   One week after finals, on a last-minute impulse, Bobby and four of her girlfriends decided to make the drive up north for the weekend. It was the dead of winter with freshly fallen snow in the Huron forest. They piled into someone's car that Friday night, and 90 minutes later stood huddled at the door of a very cold cabin in two feet of snow, in the dark, in the middle of the still woods. Shivering, they fumbled with the lock and stepped into the cabin. Bobby stuck her arm in the pot-bellied stove with a long wooden match, and coaxed the little heater to life. Almost immediately the cozy room started heating up. There was still no running water at the cabin, so they had to heat up a pot of reserve water on the stove and pour it down the pump outside in the frigid air in order to get the underground well thawed and flowing.

The five friends spent the weekend laughing, playing cards, fixing meals, and even getting their car stuck in the relentless snow, and then getting it out. They left the cabin on Sunday closer friends, with stories to tell. Bobby looked in her rear-view mirror as she pulled away from the cabin that weekend, knowing that nursing school was right around the corner; she had no idea when she'd be able to make the drive north again. She and her friends did manage to spend a couple more happy weekends toasting themselves warm by the little stove in the homey cabin.

A year later, Bobby graduated from Junior College and moved her books and notebooks to Lansing, Michigan to start nursing school. It took Bobby three years to graduate from nursing school, in 1959. During that time, she studied hard, made many new friends, but never got to leave Lansing to make the trip up north. The cabin had taken a back seat to her career, but she never forgot the woods up north and often thought fondly of the times spent there with family and friends, climbing trees as a little girl and swimming in the river.

Bobby was a good student, and got a nursing job at Bay City General. At age 26, she had grown into a beautiful young woman with a promising career. She dated off and on, but it wasn't until she met a young man named Don Berkemeier the weekend after Labor Day in 1962, that she was swept off her feet. Don was a tall, good-looking Chemical Engineer from Missouri, who made Bobby laugh and impressed her with his intelligence and kindness. He was everything she had been looking for, and Don felt the same way about Bobby. Don and Barbara were married in May 1963.

Bobby and Don, engagement party

Bobby and Don, Lake Huron, honeymoon

The young couple moved to nearby Midland, Michigan, where Don had gotten a job with Dow Chemical. Bobby quickly got a job at Midland General Hospital in pediatric surgery. She remembers vividly the afternoon that she was sitting in the break room with some co-workers; a nurse burst in the room in tears, with the news that John F. Kennedy had just been assassinated. She and her fellow nurses sat down and cried together for the fallen President; it was a moment in time she never forgot.

****

Being planners, with an eye to their future, Don and Bobby had saved up enough money to buy their first house, a small brick home on a double lot in Midland. It was the perfect starter house for a young couple, and when the front sidewalk cracked and broke, Don went out and poured new cement and fixed it himself. Their house for two quickly became a house for three when Matthew Donald Berkemeier was born in September of 1964.

Don and Bobby were thrilled with their new baby boy; they showered him with love and affection. That first year passed by so quickly, and Bobby was trying to plan a memorable first birthday for her little boy. After weeks of thinking about it, she realized that where she really wanted to be for that momentous occasion was up north in her little log cabin in the woods.

Septembers in Michigan are beautiful; the weather is still warm, the days long and lazy, and the skies deep blue, especially over the Au Sable River. Don and Bobby packed everything they needed for a birthday party for three and headed up north for a long weekend. Bobby spent the weekend introducing her husband and baby boy to her father's cabin, reliving memories and walking the much-traveled path to the river; Matthew spent the time in his mother's arms, breathing in the forest air and poking his fingers and face in a chocolate birthday cake made especially for him.

After that first trip up north for Matthew's birthday, Don and Bobby agreed they wanted to spend as much time at the cabin as possible. They bought a used pontoon boat, fixed it up in their driveway, and pulled it behind their station wagon on their way up north. They spent many weekends at the cabin, all the windows open, grilling hot dogs and gently slipping the pontoon boat into the Au Sable. Sometimes they took along a small grill and cooked on the deck of their boat as they slowly cruised along the endless miles of breathtaking river. Two years after Matthew, Jennifer Jane was born, followed two years later by their second daughter, Amanda Mary.

Don fixing up the boat

The same year that Jennifer was born was also the same year that Bobby's dear father Cliff died. She mourned for her father, who had been everything to her, a good provider and gentle teacher. She grieved knowing that her children would never get to know their wonderful grandfather, the man she looked up to and loved. Every trip up north brought with it memories of her father; every time she unlocked the front door she thought of him. Bobby felt strongly in her heart that her kids should have the same experiences that she'd had, growing up looking forward to those weekends at the cabin. She knew she wanted to continue the tradition that her parents had started with her and her sisters. Bobby made a promise to herself to pass along the cabin experience to her children and grandchildren.

Don, Helen, Cliff, Matthew

****

Helen, Bobby, Jennifer, Annie, Matthew, Shirley

When the Berkemeiers made their trips up north, the station wagon would be packed to overflowing. They were now a family of five with a boat, life jackets, a cooler, suitcases, baby blankets, books, and games. They enjoyed their summers up north so much that they began to wonder what it would be like to spend a few winters up north as well.

The Huron Forest during winter is a vast, silent expanse of towering evergreens and thick snow. From November to February, the woods are covered in a white glistening blanket; the animals hibernate, except for a few small chickadees and juncos. The river freezes over; long sparkling icicles hang from branches and gutters. When winter comes to the woods, people pull their boats out of the water, take down their summer docks, and close up their cabins for the season. The hearty winter sportsmen take over; the woods are full of ice fishermen, cross-country skiers and snowmobilers. The Corsair ski trails stretch on endlessly, and are rated some of the best trails in the country. Skiers glide along for hours and never hear a sound or see another human being.

After their second child was born, Don and Bobby bought a Ski-Doo snowmobile, a bright yellow one with a black stripe down the side. It didn't go very fast, which was fine with them. They also bought a small cart that attached to the back of their new machine, in the same bright yellow with a black stripe. The first chance they got, they pushed it up on to their trailer and soon were driving up north to be the first Hale family to use the cabin for a winter getaway. The snowmobile added a whole new dimension to their lives. Bobby could now take her family up north to the cabin in the winter, too. The car was even more fully packed on those cold-weather trips, with all the down coats, extra socks, and snowmobile suits for the kids.

The cabin in winter

The first time they used the snowmobile, Bobby was nervous; she had 3 young children all climbing aboard a machine that was soon going to be zipping up and down bumpy trails, miles away from civilization. Don climbed in at the driver's seat, with Matthew wrapping his arms tightly around his daddy's waist from behind. Bobby sat in the cart in the back, one arm around each of her daughters. Don gave the Ski-Doo some gas and off they went, down the cabin road a different way than they'd ever been, on a snowmobile.

Matthew, Jennifer, Amanda, Bobby

The snowmobile was a big hit; they loved the fast rides through the glistening, icy snow, faces getting a cold spray at every turn. Bobby began to look forward to those winter weekends as much as their summer ones. Don always drove the snowmobile, and as the kids got older and he got more daring, he would drive faster, even accelerating down steep hills which made Bobby close her eyes and pull her daughters closer to her in the cart. Soon they got in the habit of making hot chocolate and bringing it along in a couple of thermoses, which they would pass around when they'd stop for a break on the trail. They would pull up to the cabin door after a long afternoon in the cold, tired and with stinging red cheeks. Bobby would open up the cabin and the little warm room would greet them. The kids would immediately start to peel off their suits and wet mittens and scarves, and Bobby followed around after them, picking up the little items and placing them on the stove to dry. Everyone would get on their warmest sweatshirts and curl up in one of the big chairs to read or sleep. That was the time when Bobby would start making dinner, usually something warm and filling, spaghetti being the favorite dish on those cold winter evenings. Bobby cooked dinner while Don watched the kids, and she always found herself reflecting on the day spent with her family, thinking back to the times when she herself came up to the cabin as a young girl, walked in the woods with her father and shot a rifle off the back porch steps.

Jennifer and Amanda

In 1969, the frequent trips up north for Bobby and her family came to an abrupt end when Don took a management position in Rhode Island. They weren't sure when they'd get to see the cabin again; they moved out east with many memories of their place in the woods. The position in Rhode Island lasted about eight months, then Don got transferred down to Tennessee. They enjoyed the rolling hills, friendly people, and slower pace of life; even though Bobby didn't voice it too often, she missed the Michigan lakes and rivers and the little cabin.

Don's next job opportunity came two years later, and brought them back up to Michigan, on the west side of the state in St. Joseph. It would be a longer drive for them, but they couldn't wait to go back up to the cabin. Their new home was a short drive to the St. Joseph River; they didn't waste any time, and as soon as summer came to St. Joe, they spent every Sunday after church slowly cruising up and down the beautiful winding St. Joe River, grilling burgers on the front deck of their pontoon boat. As the kids got older, they even got to take turns driving the boat, with their father close by. Often they stopped and dropped anchor at an inviting turn in the river, and all would jump in the clear water for a cooling swim, the kids dipping under the big pontoons and swimming in the eerie shade of the wide boat.

Their first summer back in Michigan, Don and Bobby loaded up the sleek station wagon once again, and made the now longer trip up north to their cabin. Bobby thought the grass looked a lot longer and the pine trees next to the cabin much taller, but the rest of the memories were the same. The same smells drifted from the woods as they drove down the bumpy lane; the sandy river was still clear and clean; the cabin welcomed them just as it always had.

It was good to be back.

The family started their winter trips up north again too, just as if they never left. The snowmobile had sat idle during their time in Tennessee, but it started right up again with just a little coaxing. More and more winter trails opened up in the Huron Forest, as the popularity of the sport grew. When the kids became old enough to go out on snowmobile adventures on their own, they rode for hours up and down gentle hills, through the flat woods, riding high on bluffs, often never seeing another living thing. The snowmobile rides always ended the same back at the cabin, with the quick peeling off of the cold, damp layers of clothes and some hot chocolate while standing around the little brown stove, and then the next child would be outside, ready to take off down the lane.

Of course the summers up north with the boat continued too, and they enjoyed the Au Sable River every time they made the trip. They often invited friends and family to go with them, providing life jackets and enough hamburgers, sodas, and potato salad for everyone. Even when the boat was not in the river and was sitting next to the cabin on blocks, the kids would go outside and climb up the ladder and pretend to drive it, sitting in the chairs and pretending to be on a fast ride down the river.

Steve Ahrens, Bobby, Jennifer, Julie Ahrens, Amanda, Matthew

In 1978, Don and Barbara did end up moving back to southeastern Michigan, when the kids were in middle and high school. The kids were busy with their friends, with studying, and with school sports, and so trips to the cabin were at a minimum. They made the drive once or twice a summer for a nostalgic weekend of walking through the woods and swimming in the river.

It was around this time that the Hale sisters decided to put running water inside the cabin. They all knew the outhouse and the old hand pump out front were items of nostalgia and would be missed, but everyone quickly adapted to the little sink with hot water in the corner of the kitchen, and the tiny bathroom in the space that used to house life jackets.

Years passed and the Berkemeier kids grew up, got married; one moved away. They graduated college and got jobs. They made new friends, got married and moved to new neighborhoods. For a time, the cabin took a back seat to new pastimes and pursuits. It wasn't long though, and all three kids, now adults, eventually found themselves back up north in their hiking shoes and flannels, sleeping in the big bunk beds of the cabin.

Today, hot water on demand has now become standard at the cabin (even if the faucet leaks and the water is a little rusty). We all agree making those updates was money well spent. There are plans in the works to have a small shower installed, displacing another small closet filled with old jigsaw puzzles and folding lawn chairs. While we all welcome these modest modernizations to our cabin, we all are also in agreement on another item: no one wants a phone line put in any time soon.

****

More than thirty years later, the Berkemeier family, both kids and parents, still make their way up north to the cabin as much as possible. Matthew got married and moved away first to Boston and then to Utah, over fifteen years ago. He now has two young girls, neither of whom had ever been to the cabin, but had heard many stories about it. A few summers ago we planned a Berkemeier reunion up at the cabin over the long Fourth of July weekend, and were thrilled when Matthew said he'd come from Utah and bring his two daughters, Kristen and Lauren.

Don, Bobby, Matthew and his girls drove up north on a Wednesday, and I drove up on that Friday afternoon, having gotten a half day off work. It was wonderful to be up north in the hot sun with my family, and especially to see my brother there after a 20 year absence, reliving the old childhood memories, of which there were many.

I arrived at the cabin in the late afternoon and opened the door of my little truck, letting out my two very anxious dogs. Unloading the truck of groceries and a duffle bag, I rounded up the dogs and we all stepped inside the cabin. After the usual hugs and greetings I sat down at the big kitchen table for some pink lemonade and conversation. I watched my mom bustle around the tiny cabin, fluffing pillows and making jokes. She seemed unusually happy. Watching her, I became curious about what was making her laugh so often and seem so pleased. Then I glanced over at the huge cabin couch covered in an old quilt; her two granddaughters on the couch in their matching shorts, hair in pigtails, their perfect chins in their little hands, lying on their stomachs and reading the same comic books that my mother used to read, years and years ago.

85

Bobby, Au Sable River

Janie Hale

Janie Hale

Bobby Hale loved having a room to herself on the second floor of the pale green house on South Chilson. Winter turned to spring in 1939, Bobby turned three, and Cliff and Helen began to shuffle things around in the girls' upstairs bedrooms. On March 7, Jane Countess Hale was born; Bobby had a tiny new roommate.

Janie was the last of the Hale sisters; she rounded out the family. She grew into a sweet girl with big blue eyes, light blond hair, and a quick friendly smile. Janie and Bobby shared a room, all their clothes, and grew up together became best friends. They played together, told secrets, laughed at private jokes, got angry at each other and made up. They took turns setting the table, cleaning the house, and helping daddy out in his backyard garden. Janie liked to wear her long blond hair in two braided pigtails, and Bobby would braid it for her upstairs in the little bedroom they shared, using the light of the early morning sun coming through the dusty window. The floorboards would creak as they played their imaginary games of horses or dolls, or a game of jacks; girlish laughter floated down the stairs as their mother fixed dinner. The wooden stairs would pound as they'd race down to be the first to the table when dinner was called.

Janie loved life and she laughed often; she was part of a loving family that shared many happy times together. When her mother and father decided to build a cabin up in the woods, her life suddenly got even better.

Janie remembers dinner-table talk about a cabin being built for her daddy and his best friend, somewhere up north. The Hales were a family of modest means, content with just being together and with the simple things in life. They were not a family that could afford big vacations or to spend money lavishly; the little cabin being built in the woods was a once-in-a-lifetime endeavor. The excitement in the Hale house was tangible whenever someone talked about the construction that was going on up in the woods on their little lot. Janie had an imagination that knew no bounds, and in her young mind she saw a huge forest with wild animals, blue skies by day and deep dark woods by night. By the time the building started and progress was being made, she felt like she couldn't wait another day to drive up to the woods and see their new cabin.

That first drive up north seemed to take forever; in reality, it was just a 90 minute drive. The Hale family pulled into their small lot in the Huron Forest, bumping over the uneven ground, driving around tree stumps and deep ruts. Uncle Bill's trailer had settled in nicely to the right side of the lot, and his little dogs had made the woods their home. The family of girls and proud parents piled out of their car, the four sisters racing to hug Bill and then climbing up on to the floor of the cabin and exploring the piles of sawdust.

In early summer, the cabin wasn't a cabin yet; on that first visit the girls explored a square dusty floor, stacks of freshly cut timber and well-worn tools lying around. When they were done imagining where the rooms and kitchen were going to be, they moved off into the cool Huron Forest and got their first taste of the birch trees and evergreens that they would come to love.

Weeks went by, and the weekends up north became familiar. The men spent their time in friendly debate over how the cabin should be constructed; ultimately they always agreed with each other and rolled up their shirt sleeves, picked up their tools, and began to saw and hammer, sweating as the day heated up. Janie, Bobby, Judy Thomas and their mothers took slow, lazy walks down the dirt road to the Au Sable River, to dip their feet in the warm water. They sat in the sand along the river bank, getting up only to skip stones under the hot sun. In the evenings they all drove the short distance down to the Clements, who served a big dinner for their friends and then made up the extra beds and couches and even floors on which the Hales to get comfortable for the night. When dawn broke Janie lay still on the floor with her eyes open, hardly able to wait for someone else to get up so she could too. In keeping with true Midwest hospitality, Emma Clement made extra room at her big kitchen table for her friends, and everyone got a huge amount of home-cooked breakfast before they set out again down the road for another day of basking in the sun and building a cabin.

Janie loved her first trip up north, and each time they made the drive, her affection grew. Construction was further along with each successive trip; as they bounced down that final dirt road, they could see the progress – a partial wall in place, a bedroom mapped out. On a hot Friday in late August, the Hales again drove up to the cabin site. Janie looked over her daddy's car seat in front of her, and through the window she thought she could see beds already built through the frame of the cabin, sitting in what would eventually be the bedrooms. She was right. Uncle Bill had built two solid wood full-size bunk beds on opposite sides of the cabin, before the walls were finished and the ceiling even started.

The family spent that day in the usual way, women and children taking walks through the woods, wading in the slow-moving Au Sable, digging their toes into the sand, the men drinking beer and lemonade and hammering, sawing, and sanding. Dusk fell, and the deer began to pick their way out of the woods to feed. Cliff and Helen started to get the kids together to make the drive to the Clements for the night, when on a whim, Cliff changed his mind about where the family would eat and sleep that night. They built a fire pit in front of the cabin and cooked chicken and baked potatoes in tin foil, over the hot crackling fire that sent a thin line of smoke up into the dark blue twilight sky. They ate, sitting on the soft spongy pine needles that were thick around the cabin. Helen brought out one of her pies; strawberry dripped down dusty chins as the fire died down. They sang a few songs the girls learned at summer camp; someone yawned, eyes were rubbed, and another perfect day spent up north was coming to a close.

Dinner over and everyone full, the family washed up and threw sand on the flickering, dying campfire. One at a time, they changed into pajamas in the car, and then together stepped up onto the dusty floorboards of their unfinished cabin. Cliff and Helen gathered blankets and a kerosene lantern from the car and, smiling at each other, rolled out blankets on the floor of their brand new cabin, and kissed goodnight. Giggling, Janie followed Bobby as they curled up under blankets where their beds would soon be. Janie lay on her back and looked up at the sky, the breeze ruffling her blond hair as she rested her head on her pillow. The sky was now a deep blue-black; Janie gazed with wide eyes at the thousands of twinkling bright stars in the seemingly endless Michigan sky. The forest around the family had grown silent, except for the eerie, distant hooting owl and an occasional rustle in the leaves deep in the woods.

Janie tried to not fall asleep that night. She lay on the floor of the cabin, stretching her legs under the homemade quilt, breathing deeply. She took in the pine trees, the smoke from the dying fire, and overwhelmingly the sweet, pungent smell of freshly cut lumber of the cabin and the bunk beds. Minutes passed and she became groggy; she kept sucking in the smells until she finally drifted off to sleep on this, her first night in her new cabin.

Sixty years later, Janie says that whenever she smells the dusty, sweet smell of freshly cut wood, she is a little girl again, back on that hot summer night with the bright stars in the sky above her, drifting off to sleep on the floor of the tiny cabin with no ceiling.

Late fall came that year, and Uncle Bill was putting the final sealant on the walls of the cabin and the locks on the dark green doors; the cabin was nearly finished. Janie had spent the entire summer waiting for the weekends when she and her family would drive up north again. She loved exploring the cabin when it was being built, wandering through the framework and sifting through the sawdust; she was thrilled when it was finally done and the cabin was ready for its first hunting season.

Deer hunting was something that Cliff Hale held close to his heart, and he eagerly waited all year for November to come around. Hunting season was sacred to him, and it never occurred to him that he shouldn't take his girls out of school for two weeks, gather school lessons from teachers, and drive his whole family up north to his new cabin. And that became the family tradition during hunting season, for years and years.

Janie loved those two weeks spent up north every November, bundling up in dungarees and sweaters, wool socks and boots, helping her mother and Mrs. Thomas cook and clean. If the weather was not too cold, the women would take the short walk down to the river, and watch it flow past the dense trees now devoid of their bright autumn leaves and turning gray, the air crisp. Sometimes they'd find an old path through the forest and follow it, Janie and Bobby racing on ahead and finding a new item to collect; "collecting" became a big part of how the sisters passed their time. They would choose something and have a contest; who could collect the most pine cones, the most flat stones, the most acorns. They brought back their finds and counted them out in neat piles in front of the cabin, only to forget about them hours later as they curled up next to their mother at night as she read to them from their favorite book.

During those two weeks up north, Janie's favorite way to pass the time with Bobby was making dolls out of thick construction paper in the shape of big stars; the head of the doll was the top point on the star, and the arms were the right and left points. The clothes they made out of colored paper, or white paper that they decorated with crayons. They would add the tabs to the clothes so they could bend them over and make the clothes stay on their star dolls. They made demure evening gowns for their stars, garish jumpers and cozy pajamas, and kept all the clothes in a shoe box which was overflowing by the end of their stay.

The candy bars that her father brought up to the cabin every November were Janie's favorite. Cliff and Jack Thomas loaded up on piles of different kinds of chocolate, which they said they needed for quick energy while trudging through feet of snow in the icy forest. The two men would stop when they got winded, dig into the deep pockets of their bright orange quilted jackets and, breath coming out in puffs, would consume two or three of their favorite chocolate at a time. Janie knew about the hidden box at the cabin where the candy bars were kept; she knew she was not allowed to take one and had to wait until one was offered to her and her sister. Fortunately, Cliff bought many more than he and his hunting partner would ever eat, so Janie got a chocolate candy bar of her choice nearly every day. She would run over to the box when it was brought down from a high shelf, and standing on her tiptoes, would make her choice very carefully. She tried to eat the candy slowly but she never could; soon she'd be licking the melted smudges of dark chocolate off her fingers.

Being up at the cabin with his young family brought out the boy in Cliff Hale. For the most part, Cliff was a serious man who worked long hours at the hardware store; Janie saw a difference in her daddy when they were up north. Cliff became a man with fewer wrinkles, a man who at night pumped up the kerosene lanterns and held them up to his daughters' ears so they could laugh as they heard them hiss. He became a man who caught fireflies in old glass Ball canning jars at twilight, set them on the bedposts so his girls could fall asleep watching them ignite, then let them out after the family had fallen asleep. Cliff bought his girls ice skates up at the old store in town so Janie and Bobby could glide on wobbly legs up and down the drainage ditches that ran along Jennie Street and Cooke Dam Road near the cabin. And, it was Cliff's idea to tie up an old wooden sled to the back of their station wagon and slowly drive down the icy, snowy road to the dam, pulling one or two screaming adults and children, laughing into the wide empty gray sky as the sled slowly fishtailed to the right and the left.

Each year, as the two weeks of hunting season drew to a close, Cliff's final, heartfelt gesture was to get out his rusty axe, cut down the two fattest, greenest evergreens, haul them back to Bay City where he drove them to Janie's and Bobby's classrooms and set them up in the corner for Christmas for the school kids.

To this day, the cabin has the ability to energize, invigorate, make people loving and care-free; even the humble, hard-working man who built it was not immune.

****

Janie Hale grew up, attending middle school and high school in Bay City. She was outgoing and social, and always had many friends. She continued to go up north with her family during hunting season, and to vacation there in the summer too, as often as possible. The cabin had become a part of her; she loved the smell of the pine trees, the bright blue sky, the sense of freedom, the quiet, humble, unassuming nature of the cabin itself. She could wander for hours by herself, along the river, or she could take friends up with her and spend the hours laughing and playing cards. The cabin had become her home away from home.

Cliff and Helen attended Janie's graduation from high school in 1957. There were cheers, hugs, a few small presents, and kisses from relatives. Janie had decided on teaching as a career, and started at a local junior college that fall. She lived at home during that time, but college consumed her and instead of going up north on the weekends with her parents, she stayed home and studied. Those years sped by so quickly for her that, looking back, she found she really didn't have time to miss going to her cabin that much.

Janie finished her last two years of college in the teaching program at Western Michigan University, in the small town of Kalamazoo. While at Western she reconnected with a youn man she'd know in middle school named Tom Wood, who was also working his way through the teaching program at WMU. Tom graduated before Janie, and began looking for work. He got his first teaching job at Albion College, in a small town 20 miles east of Kalamazoo. Tom and Janie continued to date, and they found they had a lot in common; Janie loved his sense of humor, his free spirit, and his integrity. They waited until Janie graduated in 1961 to get married.

The young couple moved to Albion to be close to Tom's job. Janie started looking for work too. After one year of teaching, Tom decided teaching wasn't his calling, and he and Janie moved east to Ann Arbor, MI so he could attend law school at the University of Michigan. Janie got a job teaching kindergarten in Ypsilanti, 12 miles southeast of Ann Arbor. There they stayed for six years, Tom graduating and getting his first job at a law firm. Tom and Janie had their first child there, a beautiful, blond girl they named Laura; Janie left teaching for the full-time position of Mom. After a move and short stay in Pontiac, MI, in 1971 they ended up in Grand Rapids, which became their permanent home. Shortly after moving to Grand Rapids, the couple had their second child, another blue-eyed blond daughter, Jessica. The family of four - lawyer, housewife, two wonderful girls – had found a comfortable niche in their new town.

Janie's life had been moving at the speed of light, it seemed. Graduation, a college degree, marriage, several moves, two daughters…it all kept her very busy. In spite of looking after two young girls, Janie did have some time during her day to reminisce. Sitting in their modern kitchen and looking around her at the neat, carpeted house, the attached garage, the trim lawn and landscaping, she couldn't help but feel nostalgic when she thought of her little rustic cabin up north. Janie hadn't been up north to the cabin in years and years. Thoughts of the woods, the river, the bunk beds and the green screen doors kept running through her mind as she changed diapers, drove the girls to first days of school, and picked out outfits for school picture days. She wondered if Tom would like it up at the cabin, and one day she asked him if they could drive up some time for a long weekend, and some relaxation. They did, and while Janie loved being up north again, Tom found it almost too quiet, with not much to do. Tom loved the city life and quickly grew restless in the small cabin, with no town for miles around. The young family made the trip up north two or three times, and after that, not at all.

Janie, Jessica, Laura, Amanda, Jennifer, Tom / Rear: Don, Bobby

Tom had relatives in Tucson, AZ, and that became the place the family vacationed. She embraced his family and enjoyed the yearly trips out west, different as they were from the lazy days spent sitting in rocking chairs up north. They also spent time visiting Tom's relatives in northeast Michigan, taking the girls to the beaches near Saginaw Bay and Winona Beach. Years passed, and Janie still thought about her cabin from time to time. She wondered what it looked like, if the smells were the same, and if the river was still as beautiful as she remembered it.

Tragedy struck this close-knit family in 1981, when Tom died of complications from diabetes. His two girls were in their early teens, a vulnerable time to lose a loving father. Janie and her daughters grieved deeply for Tom, beloved husband and father.

I remember my Uncle Tom as always being funny and the life of the party, bald, with a mustache, clear blue eyes, and a motorcycle. Once, when I was five or six years old, he took me down to the shoe store and bought me the pair of red, white, and blue tennis shoes that my parents had told me I could not have. We all mourned deeply when Tom passed away; he had always been so full of life and someone whom everyone loved.

Laura, Amanda, Jessica, Jennifer

The young family struggled through the next year, each trying in their own way to deal with Tom's death. Laura and Jessica grew closer, turning to each other for support and companionship. Janie met Walt VomSteeg, who worked at the Toyota dealer in town, and they were married two years later.

Janie and Walt both loved the outdoors and especially animals. A few years after they were married, they bought a beautiful old farmhouse on twenty acres on the outskirts of Grand Rapids. Janie and Walt put in many hours updating their historical farmhouse with the big bay window and piano room, barn with work area, and chicken coops that needed mending. They bought a horse for their Laura and Jessica, who loved to ride, and were busy for years on the show circuit, jumping and showing in equestrian classes. They got a Golden Retriever who sat on their back porch and barked whenever someone pulled into their gravel circular lot, and who slept at the end of their bed at night. Janie and Walt found their barn had come with many barn cats, who somehow quickly found their way into the main house. For extra income, Janie began working part time at a tack store where the girls took riding lessons, selling fine leather saddles and bridles to other young riders.

The years were passing by, and Janie found herself busier than she had ever been.

****

The 1980's were drawing to a close. Janie's girls had grown up, said good-bye to the beautiful old farm, and gone off to college. Her life was not exactly slowing down but, with the girls gone and no more horse show circuit, she did finally have some time to think about just maybe taking a vacation somewhere. Janie's first thoughts were about the cabin, however she kept dismissing them, as Walt suffered from painful bouts of arthritis, making it nearly impossible for him to make the 5 hour drive in the car; he would find it very difficult to go on any walks in the woods if he was even able to get there. Frustrated, she tried to find a solution; she had become determined to get up to her cabin again. Finally, she asked Walt if he thought he could manage the feeding of the horses, cats, dogs, and chickens on his own, if she were to find some time to get away. He told her to go, that he would take care of things at home.

Janie then had to convince her sisters to make some time for a trip up north with her. Bobby, Pat and Shirley were all going up every now and then with their families, but they also had busy lives. It took Janie years of pestering them with the proposed trip, until a long weekend began to take shape. They decided to make it a fun girls' weekend with the men staying home. Because of Janie's persistence, the first annual Girls' Weekend at the cabin took place in the early 1990's. The four sisters invited all the female members of the extended Hale family, and in all parts of Michigan the women were taking half and full days off work to make the trip up north. Everyone wanted to go during the fall color change which, along the Au Sable River, is legendary. It was agreed that the get-together would be the third week in October.

That first trip there were eight women, everyone bringing bags of food, warm clothes, board games, sleeping bags, binoculars, cameras and blankets. The first arrivals got dibs on the bunk beds, and the rest took the couch or blankets on the floor. Janie's two dogs and Pat's orange tabby cat rounded out the group.

Janie had planned the big trip, and because of last minute things at home, was one of the last to arrive. It was a crisp, fall day; Janie finally pulled up in the late afternoon on that Thursday in October. She stepped slowly out of her little station wagon in front of the cabin and stretched; 5 hours in the car was a long time and she was stiff. It had been many years since she'd seen her log cabin, since she'd walked along the river, since she'd smelled the forest pines. Her sisters all had gotten there before her, and someone had put a pot of homemade soup on the stove. Janie opened up

96

her trunk and pulled out her suitcase, the apple crisp she'd made and the cupcakes she'd bought. She heard muted laughter from inside; her sisters had already settled in around the big kitchen table and into the big rocking chairs. Janie stood still and took a deep breath of that Huron Forest air and it all came back to her in a moment; she was finally back to her home away from home.

Bobby and Janie, Au Sable River

****

The Girls Weekend at the cabin is now an annual event. We plan it at the same time every year, around the third week in October. This is the time when the colors along the winding dirt roads are brilliant; unbelievable stretches of deep red, dusty yellow and dark burgundy. We take endless walks in the woods with our dogs, build campfires and make s'mores, and follow old trails along the river. We each bring enough food to feed ten people, and this is the week we all splurge, so we end up with a cupboard full of everyone's personal favorite indulgences: M&Ms, chocolate cupcakes, cheese curls and Cheez-Its, ice cream and candy corn, to name a few. We take turns cooking dinner, and whoever is the first one up makes the coffee in the morning. It is a week we all look forward to, and this time spent together at our little cabin, which holds so many memories for all of us, never lets us down. No matter what we have going on in our lives, we always try to make this trip to spend time with those we love.

Pat, Shirley, Bobby, Janie

PART THREE

GOODNUFRUS

Matthew and Jennifer at the old hand pump

Everyone I know who lives in Lower Michigan has a place to go "up north". We Michiganders flock there in the summer for the beaches, bluffs, sunsets, fishing, water sports, hiking, and canoeing. We take our boats, ORVs, campers, tents, mountain bikes, and dogs. We go in the fall for the colors and unparalleled photo ops. In the winter we make the trek up north to snowmobile, cross-country ski, or even dog-sled. The lucky ones have a place of our own to which we escape up north, a family cabin, cottage, or second home. The next best thing is to have the in-laws' or best friend's place to use. The rest have found favorite beaches or spots in the woods to rent cabins or homes year after year.

Whatever the reason, wherever we end up, we go up north year-round by the carload.

Not too long ago I read an article in a Michigan publication that posed the question "where is 'up north?'" Readers were encouraged to write in their opinions on the subject. Most people cited certain geographical lines across the state of Michigan and stated that "up north" is north of this line, or north of a certain city.

"Up north" is a state of mind. It is a place we reach once we get to our destination, once we have unloaded the coolers and beach clothes, and stocked the refrigerators and cookie jars. It can be one hour's drive away; it can be six hours away. There is no true geographical location.

"Up north" can be anywhere for anyone. What is the same for us all though, is how we feel once we're up there. It's that feeling we have after we've been there for five minutes, and even better, after a few days. It's freedom, adventure and peace of mind. It's how we feel when we know we have to come back too, that sense of longing as we leave "up north" behind.

Tell anyone in Michigan that you're going "up north" on your vacation, and you won't need to explain anything further. Tell someone who doesn't live in Michigan, and you will be going into detail about the city you're driving to, why you're going, what you're taking and what you're planning on doing.

To a Michigander, it doesn't matter where we go up north, as long as we make sure and get there.

THE JOURNAL

Thanks to Aunt Shirley, the friends and family who have visited the cabin have been keeping a journal of their visits since 1979. The first people to see the empty new notebook pinned to the wall of the cabin found this note from Shirley:

"ESSENTIAL. Please sign your names and the dates you were here. And a few comments too, if you feel so inclined. Like did you see any deer? What was the weather like? Did you have a good time?"

The first entry in the journal is dated 8/26/79, and is in my childish 13 year old handwriting; very uncomfortable cursive with big circles over the "i"s instead of dots. I wrote, "The kitchen counter looks nice! We had a nice time! Hi Aunt Shirley!"

Someone else added "Put skirt around cupboard." And then, in my mom's neat cursive writing, "Washed potholders and dresser scarves, couch and chair covers."

Fortunately the journal entries became more complete and colorful with each visitor, and now we have six full steno pads filled with the details and memories of short weekend visits and wonderful, relaxing weeklong stays up at the cabin by cousins, brothers, sisters, dads, moms, aunts, uncles, and friends.

CHAPTER ONE

The More the Merrier

From the Journal...

February 29, 1980; Carl, Bev, Pam, Bill & Billie, Becky & Marty (friends and family) – "Decided on spur of the moment to come up north. It doesn't take long to pack. Friday night was started with a game of 'Pig Mania' by the stove (so we could stay warm); dumb game!! Sat went for walk to dam and back. Very enjoyable. Enjoyed watching blue jays fighting for popcorn and bacon grease."

Friday June 20, 1986; Pat Ahrens (?) – "Been fishing with much <u>success</u> all week – now have <u>50</u> fish for our 'super super' fish fry tonight...all cleaned by Shirley, all 50 of 'em."

Sept 5, 1987; Barb, Jennifer & friend Kris, Don & Amanda – "Finished the puzzle, and now it's time to leave...had such beautiful weather. Saw 4 deer, 1 weasel and two strange birds...also saw 17 all-terrain vehicles, 4 motorbikes, 29 speedboats..."

Sept 24, 1988; Pat, Bobbie, Shirley – "Lovely weather! Great sleeping! Ready to tackle the upholstery problems. Emily and Lloyd said we just missed seeing Judy Thomas..."

June 11, 1990; Shirley, Pat, Crickie, Bill, MaryAnn, Mason the dog – "So far we've caught 26 fish – we need more for a fish fry! We got more, 36 fish... Shirley cleaned and cooked all the fish. She's the greatest. MaryAnn didn't want to fuss with the little bones so she just ate sweet corn & salad (lettuce from Emily's garden)...It rained all day Saturday. The ladies went to town and had hot fudge sundaes. We snacked every 30 minutes. Annie bought a hat".

Oct 13, 1990; Jennifer, Steve, friends Jamie, Jeff, Michelle, Jill – "Arrived around midnight…sat up and played cards and had fun. Saturday around noon MaryAnn, Bonnie and dogs arrived with canoe…Saturday afternoon around 3:30 a wayward soul named Jill wanders in with only a case of beer and good nature to offer. Breakfast was served about 4pm. Oct 15, we've had such a nice weekend…MaryAnn is simmering a big pot of chili, and we'll have corn on the cob & hot homemade bread, the bread courtesy of Emily next door (yum)! Also fresh-picked mushrooms from next door."

September 27, 1994; Jennifer & Calvin – "Here on our honeymoon & having a great time. Steve & MaryAnn were wonderful enough to surprise us with a basket full of goodies – champagne, chocolate, bath niceties, candles, and champagne glasses!"

August 4, 1995; Amanda & Kurt – "It's been so long since I've been up here…maybe six years…Now I can't believe I'm up here for the first time with my husband of three years…And how blessed we all are to have a place we love so much that holds such nice memories for all of us."

July 10, 1996; Laura & Tom – "Tom & I would just like to thank you all so much for everything. The cabin was so welcoming (and we loved the helpful hint notes!), and thank you for the great surprise treats! MaryAnn and Steve, thank you so much for the lovely basket…Thank you Annie for the yo-yos!… And thank you to everyone for the gift certificate. We had a wonderful dinner on the lake. And thank you all for sharing our wedding with us."

August 16, 1996; Jennifer, Jill & husband Pete – "Hi it's Jill (Jennifer's friend) up here with a little suggestion. Since you have a microwave and television up here, I think someone should bring an automatic dishwasher so I don't have to watch my good friend Jennifer do the dishes every day!"
"I am Pete. I like up north. My jeep got dirty, but we all laughed so it was a good thing. I liked the siren too."

June 6, 1997; Annie and Shirley – "Annie and Shirley here to open cabin. Just like the old days! Couldn't get the hot water going, so hauled in water in pails. Bonnie and Carol came up for one night but they didn't seem to mind the pail detail…On Saturday we went in to Tawas – Ben Franklin's – bought ourselves new sweatshirts…"

August 17, 2001; Jennifer & Amanda – "The 'mattress weekend'. No more saggy mattresses (we replaced the originals that came with the cabin)... brought all 3 dogs...The dogs were good if we take an average of all three; they love the water. Ate at Desi's Friday night and grilled steaks on the grill Saturday..."

September 14, 2001; Jennifer, Amanda, dogs Brindie, Jasper, Lucky – "Brindie apologizes for pulling off the table covering on the wash basin, pulling it into her crate and tearing it to shreds..."

October 10, 2002; Jennifer, Amanda (with dogs), Pat, Crickie, Shirley, Janie, Annie, Bobby, Mary, Marguerite, Don – "Fall colors just starting... Campfire with chili down by the river...Full cabin!...Watched movie and then figured out where everyone would sleep...Highlight was the campfire at the river. Janie brought a buffet table; Crickie gathered flowers & ferns and fall leaves for the bouquet. Pat made chili...We also had tiki torches to help keep the mosquitoes and bears away. We roasted marshmallows..."

MY BROWN EYES BLUE

Journal entry – August 8, 1993
  Laura

"Laura arrives!...No one else is here next door on either side. Went to Oscoda to Glen's to get groceries...On the way I bought my fishing license at the Dam Store...I brought my VCR just in case but it doesn't hook up. Just as well I guess. Wednesday night was the meteor shower and I went down to the river by the dam and sat on the car and watched at about 10:30 pm. It was amazing!"

August 13
"Jennifer and her friend are coming tonight. Will write more then."

"Yum. Leftovers! Still no sign of Jennifer & friend..."

"This is a great place."

"Jennifer and Jill arrived about 10:30 pm, bringing food and cheer. Today they made us go on a 20 mile hike through giant hills when it was 95 degrees. It was...really fun...We went across to the point in the boat. Jill drove and it took 45 minutes to get across. Campers gathered at the edge of the river to chuckle good heartedly at her folly. We cooked Aunt Bobby's steaks, garlic bread, and zucchini and squash...they tasted great because we cooked them ourselves on an open fire. I ate squash (don't tell my mom)."

Jill and I loved those weekends up north. Spring would come and then summer, and we'd start to get that outdoor itch to get away from the 9-5, the fluorescent world, the skirts that had become too tight and the endless customer service efforts. A quick phone call to Jill: "Let's go up north" was all that was needed; the rest was understood. All that needed to be done was pick the weekend.

This trip up north started like all the others in the past: I'd watch the clock at work (more so than usual), and come three thirty my heart would be racing a little and my mind was wandering wildly. I'd tick off my mental list of items to take on the trip, again. By five o'clock the computer screen would be blank and already faded from my memory by the time I started my car out in the office parking lot.

I drove over to Jill's house that early Friday night, already feeling liberated in my jean shorts, t-shirt and tennis shoes. I pulled into her driveway, narrowly missing the huge cooler that accompanied us on every trip to the cabin. The big red cooler was surrounded by charcoal briquettes, a backpack, a few sweatshirts, Jill's giant purse, and a boom box. I smiled; Jill was ready.

I jumped out of my Probe and opened up the back hatch, shoving my stuff to the side to make room for the big red cooler. Jill came out of the house, Pepsi in one hand, cigarette in the other.

"Hey you", I shouted. "How's it going?"

"Good. I'm SO glad to be going away. I hate work".

I agreed with her.

"What do we need to get?" Our trips up north always started with the necessary trip to the closest party store, for the essentials.

"Beer, ice, pop, snacks...should we get some vodka?"

"Mmmm, well, we're only going to be gone for the weekend. I'll stick with just beer."

"Ok, that's cool."

We spent the next few minutes shoving things in my trunk, and for all the random shoving, it was actually pretty neat back there when we finally slammed down the hatch. Jill made one last trip through her house to check for anything left behind, locked the door and we backed out of her driveway, the radio cranked up.

We stopped at the first party store we saw, and we walked in like a couple of party store pros: guerilla shoppers, we were in and out. She grabbed her pop and snacks, I grabbed mine. We met up at the beer aisle.

"What kind of beer do you want?" she asked me.

"I don't know...let's see..." I was about to start making some suggestions when Jill said "Hey, how about THIS? Have you ever seen this before?" She was holding up a six-pack of Bad Frog beer, made in Michigan. I stepped closer to look at the unique label and noticed that the cartoon-like frog on the label was holding up his middle "finger" to anyone who paused long enough to check him out. "The Amphibian with an Attitude" was printed underneath. Jill and I giggled and grabbed a case; we had our beer for that weekend. We paid for our things and made our case of Bad Frog very comfortable in the cooler in the back. The radio was cranked up again as we headed north.

The three-hour drive up north is always a quiet and dreamy one; it's the anticipation of what awaits at the end of that final dark, forested, dirt road. You begin to shed your usual worries; stress flies out into the night. When you finally exit off of I-75 onto US 23, the windows get rolled down because you want to smell Up North (a mixture of cool fresh air, warm sand, berries, and deep dark evergreens); that means you're getting close to the cabin. Jill and I stuck our heads out of the windows and sucked in the air. Our hair whipped out behind us as we grinned at each other. The sun had just finished setting, we were feeling very full from Pringles and Combos; finally, we were closer to the cabin than we were to our jobs, traffic, and voice mail. We were feeling the first liberating tingles of our getaway.

The weekend that Jill and I had picked to go up north coincided with a weeklong visit to the cabin by my cousin Laura. Cousin Laura is a year younger than I, and we spent many a Barbie-filled weekend together as kids. I was looking forward to seeing Laura; amiable, funny, smart, laid-back, she was always a treat to be around. I had no worries about the three of us getting along famously.

Jill and I pulled up to the grassy front of the cabin around 10:30 that night. We stepped out into that beautiful, mysterious pitch-blackness that only exists in the middle of the woods, far away from the lights and residue of civilization. A couple of dimly lit lamps inside the quiet cabin beckoned us indoors. We brushed the cheesy popcorn off our fronts, swigged the last sips of Diet Coke and stepped inside the cabin. Laura was there, in her oversized nighttime t-shirt already, hair pulled back, lounging on the 7 foot long couch reading, waiting for us to get there. Our raucous greeting drifted out the screened windows and into the still night, causing the crickets to pause; sound travels incredible distances in those quiet northern nights.

After we finished with the hugging and polite family inquiries, Jill and I made several trips back and forth to the car, bringing in the mammoth cooler, sweatshirts, and half-empty bags of fried crispy foods. Out came the first of the Bad Frogs as we sat down in the overstuffed chairs to reminisce and get to know one another, old friends and new. Outside, the only sounds around us were the low hum of the cabin electricity, the crickets, and the occasional rustle of the wind in the trees.

When the long day and night finally caught up with us and we'd retired a few empties into the sink, our conversation wound down and we drifted off to the bedrooms to hunt through duffel bags for our t-shirts and hair clips. We all met out back in the kitchen for one last pretzel and a final good-night. We stood there in silence, in our bare feet on that old tile floor, munching in the dim lighting of cabin lamps.

"I love how quiet it is up here", Jill whispered softly into the room. Laura and I nodded in agreement; we had been feeling it too.

The stillness, peace and quiet are what all my guests to the cabin have loved the most about our little piece of the woods. It is one of the many things that keep us making that drive as often as possible.

Saturday morning Jill and I awoke to the incomparable smell of strong coffee brewing, blending with clean, crisp forest air. Laura had been up at the cabin for a week already and wasn't quite as tempted as we were to oversleep for hours in those big cabin bunk beds. We rolled out of our cushy mattresses, pushing back our thick downy coverings. We stretched, yawned, laughed at our hair, and ambled out into the kitchen.

"Coffee!"

It was a command, not a request. We all liked it strong and black, and lots of it.

Part of the joy of being up at the cabin and drinking hot coffee on a beautiful morning is drinking it out of the old, thick coffee mugs that have been up at the cabin forever. They are chipped, cracked, and stained with coffee but those are the mugs we all reach for when we're sitting around the huge oval kitchen table with family and friends. The only thing that made our coffee even better that morning was the generous amounts of Bailey's

Irish Crème we poured into those old mugs filled with java. We passed a pleasant morning together, opening another window with each passing fifteen minutes. The sky was completely cloudless and blue; we could smell the sand and the pine trees and I said suddenly "Let's go for a walk."

Jill and Laura protested that they hadn't quite finished their first cups of coffee. I assured them that the only thing that improves a morning walk at the cabin is taking along hot coffee in those old mugs. Within minutes, we had pulled back unruly hair and changed from our nightshirts. With fresh cups of strong coffee and Bailey's, we slipped outside the banging screen door, down the mossy stone steps, and out into the sunny Huron morning.

"Where do you want to walk?" Laura asked.

At my suggestion, we decided to walk down to Cooke Dam, and follow the river through the woods on the way back. That return trip would take us through a thick forest on a little-used path but the views of the river were worth it. It sounded like a good idea to everyone, so at the end of the dirt road we took a right towards the dam. This was a quintessential cabin walk: three girls with bed hair, flip flops, t-shirts, and old, cracked coffee cups.

The walk down to the dam is an easy one; it's a straight, flat paved road, and no more than a quarter of a mile. The three of us laughed and squinted up at the hot morning sun, throwing our desk jobs and business suits to the breeze; the laughing became louder and lasted longer the more we flip-flopped along on the hot broken pavement.

We reached the end of the road and stood looking out over the river and Cooke Dam, chatting away and letting the wind rough up our hair. I was looking forward to showing my friends the old path that cut through the woods and offered bluffs, sand and birch trees.

The views along this bluff are truly beautiful; the river peeks through the trees, glinting in the sun. I found the path and we began our slow, ambling way back to the cabin; Laura had promised to make French toast and bacon for breakfast when we got back. We stopped often to admire the picturesque bends in the river and take in the woods around us, noticing every acorn, wildflower, and flitting chipmunk. After a few minutes, we were deep in the thick of the forest; the road to our left and the dam to our rear had disappeared.

As we pressed on, I noticed that the trees and undergrowth were getting thicker and the path was disappearing. Laughing and talking, we ambled forward and lost the trail in a matter of minutes.

My friends were quick to notice: "What happened to the path??" came a question from the rear.

I was wondering that myself; it had been years since I'd been on this path. I stood for a minute looking around, not wanting to suggest we turn around and take the road back home instead. After standing confused in the middle of the thick, dense woods for a few minutes, I sensed a mutiny from Jill and Laura and made a quick decision to keep moving forward.

"Let's just keep on walking and we'll find the trail again" I said, convincing not even myself and definitely not convincing my friends. I was up for a little forest adventure but I'd had to talk my friends into just a morning walk. Laura and Jill conferred and hesitantly agreed to keep walking; against their better judgment they thought.

By now I had lost the path completely, but was determined not to turn back in defeat. I thought I could find the path again further on and headed in the general direction.

The minutes ticked on.

"Oh darn!!!" This from Jill.

"What??" Laura and I asked with some concern.

"There's a bug in my coffee. This cup's no good anymore." A deep sigh escaped Jill as she sadly poured out her beautiful cup of Bailey's and coffee.

"What a waste of Bailey's!"

We laughed a little at Jill's coffee tragedy, and for a moment it took our minds off of the fact that we truly were getting lost in the woods. We found ourselves deep in the overgrown, tangled forest with no path and only skimpy flip-flops on our feet. The woods had become too thick to push through; twigs and vines closed in around our ankles as we tripped and stumbled. I stubbornly wasn't ready to turn around though, and still felt we could make our way through the dense trees and undergrowth. We really tried, brushing branches out of our eyes, breaking off offending brush and tromping down prickly scrub with bare, white legs.

By now I too had dumped out my dirty cup of coffee and was starting to think trying to forge our own way in this forest was a horrible idea. I turned to Jill and Laura with some frustration, to suggest a change of plans;

instead the sight of them made me laugh. They looked like rogue guerilla fighters in full battle camouflage: sticky pine needles clung to their dirty t-shirts, brush stuck out of their hair at all angles and Laura had a smudge of tree sap on her cheek that had begun to collect sand. And dirty; we were all pretty dusty and sweaty.

At that moment, I began to see the humor in our situation; my sense of adventure returned, and with renewed energy I pushed forward. The day was warming up; the only sounds in the silent forest were us yelping at spiders and whimpering over a new scratch. I was wiping cobwebs out of my face and getting caught on rocks and tree stumps at every step, while Laura and Jill were grumbling and had not forgotten about the easy morning walk I had promised them. I marched on; my legs were cut and bleeding, my fingertips were covered in tree sap and my ponytail had sagged down to my shoulders.

Still no familiar signs and I was on the verge of admitting I was more than a little nervous; it was easy to get lost this deep in the woods. The sun had risen considerably in the sky since we stepped outside this morning; beads of sweat were dripping down our faces, mixing with the dust of the forest in dirty little rivers on foreheads and cheeks. Jill mentioned that the easy walk that was to take 45 minutes came and went a long time ago.

Finally, after what seemed like hours of aimless struggle deep in the woods, we came across a series of "No Trespassing" signs nailed up onto a few of the pine tree: signs of civilization. I knew that in the past few years, people had been buying up gorgeous tracts of land up here, long, lengthwise pieces along the river and building beautiful homes and cabins along the bluff. I was beginning to understand: no longer could we hikers walk the length of the river for the views; my lovely, secret river bluff path was no more and we were technically now trespassing on someone's property.

"We should turn back" Laura said, stopping with a dejected air and pointing to one of the signs.

I was still hoping to salvage the nice morning walk and I turned and pushed on, my friends not happy.

To our relief, we suddenly found ourselves in a blessed clearing; someone's back yard. And as we pushed and struggled our way onto the cool grass for a deep breath, we realized that we were being watched with some amusement and annoyance by the owners of the house having breakfast on their back screened in porch. I can only imagine what went through their heads as we emerged like forest creatures suddenly into their world; some Charlie's Angels outdoor experiment gone horribly wrong. Our t-shirts were untucked, we all had cuts on our legs and arms, our hair was sticky from tree sap and we each carried a dirty coffee mug.

"Let's GO!!!" Laura hissed.

With some guilt we waved our apologies to the residents and turned quickly, stumbling over each other on tired legs in our flip-flops. Certain of the way now, we made our way as fast as possible off of their manicured property towards the paved and by now, utterly welcome road back to the cabin.

We walked in silence until we were almost in sight of our cabin again.

"Nice short, easy walk, Jen!" Jill said, heavy on the sarcasm.

"You two are crazy" Laura said shaking her head and finally speaking, her good humor returning as we got closer to our own cabin. She turned to Jill.

"Does she make you do things like that all the time?" Jill thought about it and shrugged her shoulders:

"Hmmmmm. Sometimes", she replied.

The three of us were relieved to climb the two stone steps to our little cabin after the greatly extended and unexpected long morning walk. The cool inside of the cabin felt delicious to our hot and tired legs. Jill and I sprawled out in two of the welcoming, oversized chairs that dominate the living room in the cabin, already laughing about the walk debacle; *that* story would be told over and over and blamed on me every time. True to her word, Laura whipped up a batch of the most delicate and perfectly crispy French toast, with big slabs of bacon on the side. The smells of a home-style breakfast cooked up by a young woman who would eventually go on to become an accomplished chef drifted up through the cabin and out into the deep woods. We washed it all down with orange juice and refreshed, we were ready to have another go at the great outdoors. Jill and I did the dishes and the three of us talked about what we could do next out of doors.

There are endless walks and many touristy things to do and see in the Au Sable and Oscoda area; the activity we unanimously agreed on was a drive to the Monument and a trip down the big dune.

The Lumberman's Monument is the most famous place to stop and take a few pictures in the Oscoda area. The Monument is a giant, 14 foot tall statue built to honor the thousands of fearless, scrappy lumberjacks who helped supply lumber across the country for schools, homes, and businesses in the late 1800s. Beyond the impressive statue, a beautiful wood deck and overlook have been built, which afford spectacular views of the Au Sable as it makes one if its giant hairpin turns. Visitors who continue along the wooden walkway to its end will find themselves high atop one of the Au Sable's many beautiful, soft sand dunes. At the bottom of this steep dune are a gorgeous sandy beach and a calm swimming area. Most people stop at the top of the dune, oooh and aaah at the beauty of it, and for good reason do not attempt to go to the bottom of the dune; those who are foolish enough to give in to temptation and go down know they will have to climb back up that near vertical slope in shifting sand and blazing sun.

Jill, Laura and I reached the monument that late morning and took a quick look around the visitor area. There were a few new items in the gift shop, but nothing exciting enough to tempt us to buy. We wandered over to the overlook; I'd seen the mighty river below countless times from that spot but it still took my breath away. After pausing for a few minutes to pay that scenic vista its proper respect, we made our way to the end of the walkway and took our tennis shoes off to walk in the sand at the top of the dune, and feel the sand between our toes. There were families down at the bottom of the dune, kids splashing around in the cool, calm water far beneath us.

The three of us stood at the top, sweeping our eyes over the crystal blue river below and the deep turquoise sky with one or two smoky white clouds. It was inevitable:

"We goin' down?" Jill asked.

I hadn't planned on it but I couldn't resist the challenge.

"Definitely" I said with a quick nod of my head. I turned to Laura. "How long has it been since you've been down the dune?"

She laughed. "I have noooo idea."

"Will you be joining us?"

"Oh well, of course."

By far, the best part of a trip to the monument is running down that soft sandy dune; you can build up frightful momentum on the way down if you don't check yourself. Stopping at the bottom can be a little tricky. We clutched our tennis shoes in one hand and with a laugh sprinted off down the dune.

The slope is steep and long and with practice, you can launch yourself and land ten feet further down; much like a repeller, you can get some real air. We part ran, part leapt down the dune. We jumped, we screamed, we laughed, we gasped. In an instant, the serene family scene at the bottom of the dune was shattered, the faces of the parents expressing mild shock at the three disheveled girls with flailing arms, leaping their way towards them with little control. We hit bottom at top speed and managed to avoid running over any of the innocent children who had stopped playing in the sand to stare. Doubled over and laughing, we stood victoriously on the beach at the bottom, laughing in a circle, trying to get our breath back.

After getting lost in the woods earlier and leaping down the dune at high noon, the cool river water at the bottom was deliciously inviting. We tossed our shoes up on the beach and waded in the clear water up to our knees. We stood chatting in the caressing river water, passing nearly ½ hour wiggling our toes at the minnows that swam by and burying our feet in the cool wet sand of the river bottom. Finally, one of us suggested we'd better tackle the climb back up, so we pulled ourselves reluctantly out of the water and grabbed our shoes.

One would never guess that the beautiful dune that provided us with so much cushion, warmth and fun while charging down it, could turn so brutal on the way back up. Still laughing, we took our first steps back up the dune. After just a few steps upward, all talking amongst us had ceased, and we were breathing hard. A few more steps and we were really sucking air. Thirty more seconds of taking big steps up and sliding two steps back down, we lurched forward and began crab-walking our way towards the top. Hand hand, foot, foot. The sun found in us easy prey, and began to beat hot holes into our backs; the sweat started trickling. My legs started shaking and it quickly became a game of mind over matter.

Minutes passed in the merciless sun. I straightened up, my heart pounding, and looked back down towards the beach. I was absolutely spent and I still wasn't halfway to the top. Laura and Jill weren't faring much better; we stood randomly at three different spots on the giant dune, hair sticking to our necks as the sun beat down. I could hear Jill and Laura gasping for air too.

I tuned everything else out, the beating sun, my wobbling legs, the sand flies buzzing around my head, and concentrated only on reaching the top of that dune. When I finally made it, I nearly stubbed my toe on the wooden walkway at the top of the dune, so hard had I been concentrating on the sand directly in front of my nose.

My legs collapsed and I twisted around and landed sitting down on that welcome wooden deck. I summoned the energy to lift my head in time to see Jill and Laura make one last push and land next to me on the deck. My legs were shaking visibly. Any pretense at being in good shape was impossible.

"Well!" I said trying hard not to sound winded. "That wasn't that hard."

"That was AWFUL", Jill shot back before I had even finished my sentence.

With the remaining breath I had left I laughed.

"You're right, it was," I quickly agreed.

When our legs had stopped shaking long enough for us to shove our tired feet back in our shoes, we pushed our way into standing positions and stumbled back to the car.

We drove back to the cabin in tired silence, each of us recovering in our own way and too beat to say much. Laura may have been thinking back to a time less than 24 hours ago when she was alone and peaceful at the cabin, doing her own thing before Jill and I descended upon her.

Once back in the comfort of the cabin, each of us drifted off to relax. Reading has always been one of my favorite ways of relaxing up north. I grabbed my book, Laura grabbed hers, and Jill sat down to try to put some pieces in the large puzzle that is always in progress at one end of the huge kitchen table. It was refreshing to sit in the coolness of the shady cabin and rest tired legs. I could already feel my legs getting stiff and I knew I'd regret my bravado in all things physical the next day. The peace and quiet washed over us and I felt myself drifting off to sleep after reading only a few pages in my book. I did not fight that rare afternoon nap.

I woke up to hear the wind rustling through the trees in a late afternoon breeze. I jerked my head around to see what the others were up to; had I missed anything? Jill was just coming out of the bedroom, rubbing the sleep out of her eyes. Laura lay sound asleep, stretched out on the old couch and crumpled blanket.

"How do your legs feel?" I asked Jill in a whisper, not wanting to wake up Laura. Jill pondered my question for a minute in a sleepy daze.
"They're sore" was her answer after long deliberation.

Our hoarse whispering and poor attempts to be quiet woke Laura up, and she shook the sleepy cobwebs from her head to join the conversation. After all the exercise and fresh air, we were starting to feel hungry, and talk drifted naturally towards dinner plans. We decided to marinate steaks, take some corn and other vegetables and some baked potatoes, load up the tiny portable grill and some charcoal and take our rowboat across the river to a beautiful land outcropping we call the point.

When I was a little girl, my family used to row a small, rusty rowboat across the river over to the point every time we went up north. Sometimes we would simply row over and just enjoy new places to walk. Enterprising campers or hikers had built a fire pit on the point, and so at other times we would take advantage of someone else's good idea, and grill dinner or s'mores in addition to exploring the point.

Jill's giant cooler came in handy for our campfire dinner that night. The three of us filled it with juicy steaks, fresh julienned vegetables, baked potatoes and ice-cold beer; we filled in what remaining space was left with ice. This time, we added mosquito repellent and sweatshirts to the supplies in the trunk; even though it was a hot day it could get chilly after the sun went down on the water. Fortunately for us, the rowboat was already docked down at the gravel pit. After all the walking and hiking in the fresh air we'd done that day, our stomachs were growling and the steaks were looking good as we loaded the car and headed off to the river.

We drove the two minutes to our access spot and looked out across the beautiful river. All the fishermen were gone; the river was ours alone to row. The sandy, tree-lined point beckoned to us across the wide, slowly moving Au Sable. Gentle waves licked the shoreline as we sprayed each other generously with bug spray in the late afternoon sun. We got the cooler and our other necessities down the softly sloping hill, loaded up the rowboat and shoved off.

Laura had elected to row first; being an occasional fisherperson herself, we figured she should go first to demonstrate the finer points of rowing a rocking, leaky aluminum boat filled with stuff. She took command well, and did an impressive job of getting us halfway across the river on a nice, straight path. Jill wanted to take a turn rowing and begged to be given a chance at the halfway point. We very carefully maneuvered ourselves in the tipsy boat, coming dangerously close to dumping all of us into the clear river as Jill and Laura switched places.

Being somewhat of an outdoorsy person, I assumed Jill would know how to row a boat. Plus, there's just the plain old common sense factor that can get you a long way with two paddles and a boat. Jill had just lit a cigarette so it wouldn't do to put it out, even to concentrate on the job at hand. Not wanting the rest of her pack to get wet, she stuck her Marlboros halfway down her tank top for safekeeping. She cut a dashing picture, lit cigarette dangling from her mouth, pack of smokes scrunched down in her cleavage, turning to take stock of our destination to get her bearings. She looked so deceptively professional, so confident, so Lewis and Clark. I leaned back to enjoy the smooth cruise over to the point.

It quickly became apparent that Jill could not row a boat after all, at least not in a straight line. She leaned forward and took a big dig into the water with the oars; we lurched a bit one way, then the other, then to the left, and back to the right. This continued for several minutes.

Laura and I kept the laughing quiet at first, but we couldn't for long. Our eyes met as Jill continued to heave and row. I turned around to see where the point was; we were far off course.

"Jill!" I said sharply, "you're way off".

She jerked her head around to see, unconcerned. Back and forth we twisted, to the left and to the right. The hungry mosquitoes found in us completely helpless prey, out in the middle of the river, slowly jerking from one side to the other and making very little forward progress. Jill started laughing, which made her weak and lose the bit of concentration she had; Laura and I joined her out loud. The more we laughed, the farther from the point the little boat bobbed.

As one, Laura and I made the decision that Jill's turn at the oars was over. As funny as this was, we had almost lost sight of the point and we were hungry. We all agreed Laura should finish the trip; she and Jill carefully switched places and we quickly found ourselves dragging the little boat up onto the welcome, sandy shore of the point.

If Jill can't row a boat, she definitely can work a grill. Jill is the master griller, the queen of all barbeques. Give her some tongs, her spatula, her beer, and step back. Laura and I collected firewood while Jill made that shady clearing under the evergreens her own chef's kitchen. The thick, soft bed of pine needles was spongy under our feet as we walked around hunched over, looking for kindling and branches. It was isolated and peaceful over at the point; that's why we liked coming over here. Except for the fire pit, there was absolutely no evidence that any person before the three of us had ever been there.

We cracked open our beers, pulled up a few logs and enjoyed the smell of the steaks grilling on the open fire. The pine and birch trees made a beautiful, natural harbor around us; our improvised kitchen was a tree cave. The three of us gazed out on the silent, glassy river that was starting to turn black as the sun got close to setting. The fish were jumping in the middle of the river; we heard a loud "smack" and made it to the edge of the point in time to see beaver swimming around in the water near the shoreline. We returned to our log seats and, silently watching the river, wondered when the steaks would be ready.

Dinner that night was out of this world. The wet naps we brought proved to be invaluable as we ate like King Henry, gnawing on the dripping steaks and shoving chunks of buttery baked potato in our mouths. Plates balanced on our knees; not at all lady-like. We sat around a little fire after dinner, chatting carelessly as the bright orange sun sank behind us.

The sun dipped below the trees, spreading its bright orange glaze across the rippling dark river. Wanting to make it back to the opposite shore before it got completely dark, we quickly kicked sand on our crackling fire, cleaned up as best as we could, and loaded the cooler back in the trusty row boat. Jill did not get a second chance at the oars; she had proven herself a wonderful passenger instead. Laura and I took turns rowing on the way back.

The big dinner had mellowed us out for the trip back to shore, each of us drinking in the beautiful dusk air and trailing our fingers through the cool water. It had gotten a little cool so we put our sweatshirts on; the night air hinted at excitement still to come.

Dusk at the cabin has meant one thing to me ever since I was a young girl: a trip down the back road to look for deer. My parents used to load up the three kids in the giant, boat-like 1970 woody Ford station wagon, my brother in the front passenger seat, us girls in the back. The back road is an old dirt road that follows the power lines deep into the Huron forest. It takes you straight into the heart of the forest, so deep into it that day turns into night and that friendly dusty road becomes eerie, even on the brightest day. The road branches off at one point and follows the river atop a high bluff, making for several breathtaking scenic stops where campsites have sprung up.

When we'd first make the turn off onto the back road, Mom would slow the car down to a 5 mile an hour crawl, and we'd beg to open the windows and sit outside on the window ledges. "Ok...but you kids BE CAREFUL," she'd say. We'd race to see who could roll down their window the fastest and bounce up into the open window, our feet hanging down on the seat and the rest of us leaning out of the car. We'd grip the steel luggage rack on top of the car to steady ourselves as we'd bounce and lurch over the deep ruts on the seldom-used road. Mom would turn the lights off and off we'd crawl.

"SSShhhhh!" we'd hiss if someone made a sound.

The trick was to be as silent as possible and not scare off the deer, which came out to feed at dusk. The old car would hover along, massive and silent, like a submarine in murky waters on a covert mission. We kids were the snipers, scanning the forest with squinted eyes for any sign of our elusive white-tailed quarry. Our hearts would pound as we'd try to be the first to spot one of the shy beautiful creatures we loved.

"There's one!!!" someone would whisper, and point. Mom would stomp on the breaks and excited cries of "where??? *Where??*" would follow. The spotter would proudly point out the deer to the rest of us. By now, the deer had seen us too; three kids and an old station wagon can only be so quiet. They'd lift their heads sharply from the long grass, and stare straight at us. Their chewing mouths would stop and they'd freeze, staring at us and trying to figure us out with their huge brown eyes. Then slowly, the mouth would start moving again, finishing up the mouthful of grass. The oversized ears would start to twitch, assessing the danger. A decision would be made to either keep eating or flee. The brave ones would drop their heads and continue grazing; the timid ones would, with a quick flick of their white tail, bound off and in two or three giant, arcing leaps be out of sight, deeper in the forest, leaving us squealing with joy.

Those trips down the back road looking for deer were like going on a treasure hunt for us kids; they held the same thrill. We'd arrive back at the cabin flushed, hearts pounding and chattering about each deer sighting.

To this day when dusk falls at the cabin, my thoughts still turn to the back road and the deer. The vehicle now is an SUV; the back road is not so vacant of people; there's no hanging outside the windows, but the excitement is every bit as charged, the sight of the beautiful deer leaping away into the forest every bit as thrilling as it was over thirty years ago.

Laura, Jill and I were just finishing unloading the car and cleaning up after our grilled dinner when I suggested taking a drive down the back road. The sun had already set and it was probably too late to spot any deer but even just the drive itself along the river's bluff at night was well worth it. Still up for new adventure, my friends agreed.

We turned off on to the back road, slowing down to the required crawl. We knew we were late but we kept our eyes peeled anyway for any late deer that might be catching a last minute mouthful. Half an hour later we were deep into the thick black forest and we hadn't seen any deer; we decided to turn the car around, vowed to get an earlier start next time, and headed back towards the main road.

We were almost out of the dark forest, when about thirty feet ahead of us we noticed an unidentifiable, slow-moving creature in the middle of the road. It was low to the ground, very round, and lumbered along deliberately.

"What's THAT??" Laura asked. We squinted into the pitch darkness and began to guess. A large dog? A small bear? We sped up gradually, not wanting to scare it off but wanting to get closer. We were leaning forward in our seats, gripping the dash or the seat in front of us, whispering and guessing out loud every animal we could think of. Slowly we pulled up to within five feet of it, keeping to its snail's pace, and still it gave no indication that it even knew we were closing in. It kept up its slow, plodding pace down the middle of the dark road. Our excitement had reached a fever peak when someone finally thought to whisper, "Turn on the lights". Laura switched on the headlights, and at the same time the animal stopped and slowly swiveled a cone-shaped head around to see who was tailing it. For a full five seconds it stared directly into the headlights at us, irritated as it tried to figure us out; no one in the car breathed. This animal was completely unafraid and unconcerned at the car twenty times its size nearly on top of it. After a brief hesitation, it turned away and continued its slow, lumbering walk down the middle of the road.

It was a huge, spiky porcupine, a true warrior of the woods; this was a creature that was accustomed to getting its way, and we didn't argue. Fearlessly the heavy porcupine stayed in the middle of the road, tailed by a giant rumbling machine with bright lights and exhaust fumes. It continued its plodding walk until finally, in its own time, turned off the road and pushed its way deep into the woods and out of view.

We were thrilled; it was a rare sight, even for serious hikers or denizens of the woods. To a few girls from the suburbs, it was something to slap the back of the car seat about and keep repeating "can you believe that?"

We had talked about going in to town that night; how could we possibly top the porcupine story?

The warm glow from the old cabin lights welcomed us back as we pulled up on to the lawn after our trip down the back road.

"We goin' out tonight?" Jill asked.

"Ohhhhh yeah", was my quick reply.

Laura wrinkled up her nose. "Where is there to go?"

I turned around in mock disbelief. "You mean you've never been to the Honky Tonk Saloon??"

"Uh, no, I have NOT."

"Cousin, you are in for a rrreeeal treat."

Jill walked over to the mirror and declared she was not going out on the town without some major primping. After the dusty, sandy, gritty day we'd had, Laura was inclined to agree with her. I crowded into the small mirror and joined them. I hadn't looked or felt so dusty and woods-weary in quite some time.

I had a sudden inspiration: we were up north, far away from civilization as we knew it. Why shouldn't we go out to the saloon as we were, with no primping, no fussing, no brushing hair or straightening attire? Tonight should be one of those nights.

"No way." Jill assumed a bellicose stance, hands on hips, head cocked to one side; she was prepared to fight me on this one. I honestly didn't think my friends would go along with the idea, and they did put up some fight but after a surprisingly short battle they gave in. No one even picked up a hairbrush; no one changed their shirt, socks or shoes. We were up north, and this is how things are done.

Giggling, and with nothing to hold us up, the three of us filed out the dark green screen door and were back in Laura's car again, heading in the opposite direction this time, toward town. Moments later we were zipping along the straight empty byway, the deep Huron Forest closing in on us on both sides. I sat in the back seat and leaned forward, laughing and singing loudly along with the radio with Laura and Jill. I looked down at my scrunched up socks and straightened them out, dumping sand from the dune onto Laura's back seat. I re-tied my ponytail for the hundredth time that day as we made the turn off the main road, over the railroad tracks, and into the parking area for the Hilltop Bar and Honky Tonk Saloon.

The Saloon is located just on the outskirts of Oscoda, right before the bridge that crosses the river into town. It sits far away from the old whitewashed country churches, the Dairy Queen, the giant blue statue of Paul Bunyan, the antique stores, the hardware store, and the $2.00 movie theater. Oscoda is everything the Honky Tonk Saloon is not: quaint, quiet, friendly, and down homey. The Saloon sits shunned on the outside of town for a reason.

The dusty parking area was filled as usual with old beat up pick up trucks with gun racks. Laura looked at us hesitantly.

"This looks like a nice place" she said sarcastically.

I assured her that this steel rectangular building with no windows and beer banners hung on its exterior walls could be quite a blast. Jill agreed and we squeezed our little compact car in between a couple of rusted old road pickups. A large red sign on the door greeted us: "Absolutely NO knives". The hooting and hollering over the loud jukebox music could be heard bellowing out of the open door, held open by a big chunk of concrete. We walked in and got more than a few stares; three young, fresh faces had entered into the tired old slab stone bar with duct-taped tables and canned beer. We stood in the middle of the ruckus for a second, trying to adjust our eyes, which had been blinded by the sudden bright lights; we could barely see through the heavy fog of cigarette smoke that hung lazily in the thick, beer-soaked air. Jill spotted an empty table and we thankfully claimed it.

We sat down, glad to remove ourselves from the sales block. While we were trying to decide if there was such a thing as a waitress here, and what we were going to drink, Jill noticed someone up on the mini, foot-high stage with a load of equipment plugging in electrical wires, setting up speakers, adjusting a TV monitor...karaoke had come to the Honky Tonk!

She leaned forward tapping me on the shoulder. "Hey, look. It's karaoke night."

I had a sinister thought. I looked at Jill and said conspiratorially "Guess who's gonna get up there tonight??"

Laura knew immediately what I meant.

"NO, I am not" she said, with true menace in her voice. Laura is a classically trained opera singer and I have no doubt that she often becomes the target for karaoke requests.

"Laura" I said laughing, "don't fight it."

With me and Jill ganging up on her, and with the help of a little alcohol, quiet, shy Laura really didn't stand a chance.

Just then the waitress showed up, surprisingly good-natured despite the fact that she would spend the next four hours waiting on loud, very drunk men and women who all called her either "honey" or "doll". She took our drink order, popping her gum and fluffing up her permed, frosted hair. Jill and I ordered beers and Laura ordered a vodka cranberry. The waitress turned away towards the bar but not before I leaned over and tugged gently at her saggy tank top that was stuffed into painted-on jeans. Jerking my head towards Laura who was busy staring at the room around her, I asked in a whisper "Can you make hers a double?"

The waitress smiled at me, happy to be in on a little secret. She winked at me. "Sure honey".

The poor sap who had been hired to bring karaoke to this sea of flannel shirts and long hair finally finished testing his equipment and looked nervously around the room. No one was paying attention to him; men were arm wrestling and one guy was trying to see how many women he could get to sit on his lap. The karaoke guy began to speak tentatively into the microphone, trying to get the crowd fired up and get his first volunteer. Our waitress walked by and I ordered another round. She checked to see if Laura was looking and mouthed to me "double?" pointing to Laura. I laughed and gave her a definite nod of my head.

Anger finally made the karaoke guy take drastic measures and he signaled to the bartender to shut off the jukebox. Drunk men started to volunteer their drunk friends to get up on stage; the bulkier guys started pushing the little guys in the direction of the microphone; for a minute it seemed like a fight would break out and then everyone settled back down, with one skinny guy in tight jeans and a Smith and Wesson t-shirt left standing on the stage. To the absolute delight of the crowd, he sang his own awful version of "Sweet Child of Mine" by Guns 'n Roses, then left the stage and ran to the bar and did a shot. His performance opened up the floodgates and there began a steady stream of big burly men and their girlfriends belting out their favorite tunes.

By now, Jill and Laura and I were on our third round of drinks. I knew I had to very carefully ease Laura into the idea of singing to this crowd.

"Hey Laura" I shouted. "So, what do you think?"

"No WAY" she responded but without the same conviction as before; she actually seemed to be wavering. Was she beginning to warm to the Honky Tonk?

"This is a GOOD drink," she shouted at me over the noise.

"I told you you'd like it here" I shouted back. She sucked that drink down and, setting down her empty glass said, "Well, it depends on their song list; it depends on if they have anything in my range. I'm sure they won't, but…"

I nearly pushed Jill out of her aisle chair, urgently shouting at her to get the song list. Jill shoved her way through the crowd by the stage and came back with one. She plunked it down in front of Laura and we stared eagerly at her as she ran her finger down the list of songs doubtfully. She began sipping her third drink and, straw slipping around on her tongue, looked up at us delightedly, in spite of herself. "Well…I guess they have a few here I could sing".

Jill and I were relentless in our encouragement.

"I can't BELIEVE I'm doing this" Laura looked desperately from Jill to me as she pushed herself away from the table. We lost sight of her as she joined the milling crowd around the karaoke machines.

Two more singers went on the stage, and Jill and I eagerly and with great humor waited for Laura's turn. Laura stepped up on the platform, and Jill slugged my leg as she saw Laura fumble around with the microphone, getting ready to start. The music started, the spotlight shone on Laura, and she began to sway to the music.

I burst out laughing as I looked at Laura under the bright spotlight through the thick smoke up on the stage. Every inch of our dirty, dusty outdoors day was caked on Laura from head to toe.

"Look at her!" I shouted to Jill.

Laura had on an old tank top, stained with ketchup, a dab of tree sap on her face, cut off jean shorts with a 6 inch can of bug spray clipped to her belt; her hair had fallen almost completely from her barrettes and hung uneven over her shoulders. She had a flannel shirt wrapped around her waist and every time she took a step in her big hiking boots, sand and dust kicked up around her ankles. Streaks of charcoal marked her knees and bright red mosquito bites dotted her shoulders and thighs. The spotlight picked it all up and magnified it.

We laughed at the frightened look on Laura's face as she surveyed the rough drinking crowd just a few feet from her face. Poor Laura! It didn't matter though; no one in that rowdy loud bar was even looking at her. Then, she began to sing.

"Don't know wheeeeeeen I've been soooo blue; don't know whaaaat's come over youuuu" the first few lines to Crystal Gayle's "Don't it Make my Brown Eyes Blue".

Cans of beer clunked down on tables; men slugged each other, and told each other to shut up. The arm wrestling matches stopped, the pool games came to a halt, the inebriated couples stopped attempting to line dance by the bar.

Not only can Laura sing, she's got looks to go along with her voice. With vivid blue eyes, a petite figure, white smile and naturally platinum blond hair that many women pay lots of money for, the brawny men didn't notice the dust and saggy jean shorts.

"Whhoooo-hoooo!" "Yeah, baby!" "Sing it honey". This crowd liked her.

Jill and I were in fits of laughter. The shouting was contagious. I leaned my chair back, tilted back my head and screamed out "Go Laura!"

The large grinning man at the table next to me took up the cry.

"Laura! Laura!" he bellowed out, gulping down his beer and pounding his fist on the rickety table. The crowd joined in and soon the whole place was chanting Laura's name. Those who were not chanting were whistling; those who were not whistling were hooting. We could barely hear Laura's voice as she moved into the chorus: "Tell me no secrets, tell me some lieeees. Give me no reasons, give me alibis."

Jill and I ordered shots for ourselves to celebrate our launching of Laura's successful debut at the Honky Tonk. Her song ended amid cries of "encore!" and more "Laura!!" She pushed her way offstage and struggled through the groping crowd to collapse with embarrassed laughter into her seat.

"Gimme another drink!! I can't believe I did that". We all high-fived each other and immediately 3 drinks showed up at our table, courtesy of the table of men next to us.

We did not pay for another drink that night; Oscoda loved Laura. The smiling karaoke man announced that he had to pack it up soon, to a crowd that could have cared less. Laura suddenly felt a tap on her shoulder, and she turned around and was handed a carefully folded bar napkin. Surprised, she opened it up and written in very shaky pencil was "Can you sing 'Like a Virgin' by Madonna?" We burst out laughing, wondering which big burly man in the crowd had written *that*.

Laura didn't sing again that night; we left them wanting more. We exited the Saloon laughing and happy; every man in the place shouted "bye Laura" as we laughed our way out the door, waving. I wondered what kind of jobs these men and women would go to on Monday, and wondered how many of them would even remember shouting Laura's name at the top of their lungs to a pretty blond singer with a killer voice at the Honky Tonk Saloon.

Sunday morning was spent sipping down cups of dark black coffee and laughing about the night before. Laura was questioning what she had become, how far she had fallen. Our hair smelled like smoke and our voices were raw; nothing however that one of Laura's unbeatable breakfasts couldn't cure. Sunday was going to be another picture perfect day, but was unfortunately also the day that Jill and I had to head back down to our jobs and paperwork.

We finished the dishes and each wandered off lazily, still groggy from the night before and now weighed down by omelets, bacon and potatoes. Jill shuffled her way with her coffee into the bedroom, opened up a window and I heard her pick up her book, roll into bed and yawn. Laura stretched out on the giant couch that someone had supported with cinderblocks in the middle. I found my way to my favorite chair at the cabin, a huge, overstuffed rocking chair that is big enough for an adult to curl up comfortably in and fall asleep. That's exactly what I had in mind as I opened up the window next to the chair and, wrapping my bathrobe around me and curling my knees up under me, leaned my head back on the welcoming old soft chair that my grandfather used to sit in.

In the silence of the late morning we all drifted off to sleep; hard to believe we'd arrived just 36 hours before. In that amount of time, we'd hacked our way through a wild, overgrown forest, leapt and screamed our way down a mountain of a dune on the prettiest river in Michigan, stared down a porcupine and readily admitted defeat, and tamed a smoky room filled with rowdy drunk mechanics and lumberjacks. But the most important thing we'd accomplished in those 36 hours, was what Jill and I had set out to do when we packed our trunk full of weekend cabin things; we'd gotten away from the city, away from our jobs, forgotten the smell of exhaust and lived stress-free. Even if just for a short period of time, we'd done it. We knew as we drove back down home, that the cabin would still be there for us the next time we needed it, when we needed to come up for air and shake off the world for a while.

Au Sable River dunes

CHAPTER TWO

Getting our Groove Back

From the Journal...

October 8, 1979; Mary, Jim, Pam, Annie (friends/relatives) – "Came for a walk in the woods and to see the colors. Pam ripped her pants...Annie sipped cocoa...what a nice way to spend your day off!"

June 25, 1980; Mary and Cathy W. (old friends of the family) – "Cabin sure was a beautiful sight on arriving...curtains, counter top and skirt are very pretty...maybe 24 or more years since I was last here...things have changed so much around here...sure is lovely..."

Wed June 12, 1986; Shirley Causgrove – "Arrived alone about 4:00pm after driving through the <u>worst</u> rain storm ever! Got everything inside and finally got cabin warmed up. Tried pump but got soaked. Thurs – Rain again today. Still puzzled about pump – got soaked again... Fri – Finally got pump going!!!!!! Shirley extremely happy and very modest about it all."

Aug 20, 1989; Unknown – "...I was in Saginaw I thought I'd spend a week up here in peace & solitude, no phones, no TV, no nothing. Arrived about noon in the pouring rain. It rained all day but peaceful. No phones, no TV, no nothing. Fixed stove.

MON. Beautiful day. Went fishing in several places. No phones, no TV – no fish!

TUES. Rain again. Spent the day in the cabin. EGAD! No phones, no TV, no nothing! Maybe I wasn't cut out to be a hermit.

WED. Bored. NO PHONES, NO TV, NO NOTHING. Guess I'll eat, and clean the cabin. If I still feel like it I'll head for home..."

Oct 5, 1990; Don & Bobby – "Got up here about 11:30 pm…trees almost peaked. Don ran while I had my toast & coffee (better than running)… Sunday, cold (46 degrees) and rainy, even though the weatherman promised 80 degrees and sunny. Oh well, we enjoyed it here anyway. Can't complain when you've had homemade chicken noodle soup for lunch."

October 1990; Bonnie (friend) – "It's been great from the minute I left South Haven, being with Steve and MaryAnn, my best friends…The colors are breathtaking. The deer eating in the back yard, wild turkey. Even the shower on the back porch was great, cold but warm. We don't want to leave but that's the way it is."

October 29, 1991; Crickie – "Had two peaceful days alone before closing the cabin for the winter. Long walks in chilly weather, finished the puzzle, watched the World Series (Twins beat Atlanta). Quiet, comfortable; cabin is great for solitude…"

August 11, 1993; Laura – "Yea, no bat…I walked around cautiously for a few minutes making sure, since I am alone…no one else is here next door on either side. Went to Oscoda to Glen's to get groceries…I brought my VCR just in case but it doesn't hook up; just as well I guess. Wednesday night was the meteor shower & I went down to the river by the dam and sat on the car & watched at about 10:30 pm. It was amazing! They looked like fireworks…"

August 23, 1994; Mary Roeder, Henry Roeder – "Hi all. Henry & I came up for the good old days." "Hello all, visiting from Germany and wanted to see the ole cabin and remember the good times. Great to find it in its original state. Wish all of you the best and have a great time."

October 6, 1995; Jennifer and friend Jill – "It is so nice to be able to stop, sit back, watch nature in her glory and smell her perfume. (Much nicer than to stop, watch for the green light & inhale CO_2).

June 27, 1997; Jennifer – "It's Jennifer up here by myself for the first time (though I've thought about it many times!). I'm not really alone though because I brought my beautiful dog Lucky…Last night was gorgeous, I got here just in time to go to the gravel pit for sunset…I'm enjoying my second cup of coffee and a bagel."

September 30, 2000; Jennifer, dog Lucky, cat Nero – "*Arrived this morning around 11am, Lucky, Nero and I. I am up for 5 days or so; have already left the corporate world far behind…Went into town for groceries, went to Carter's and then a few doors down to the German/Bavarian bakery…found out where the best pizza place in town is as well as the video store…I'm cooking my steak & potatoes…Stove is a little slow; that's ok, I definitely have the time.*"

June 22, 2002; Jennifer, dogs Lucky and Brindie – "*Arrived Friday night after work…It sure is dark up here at night; glad to have the two dogs with me…read my book for awhile, as I was wide awake, due to the double espresso I slammed before I hit the road…Saturday morning took the dogs for a walk to the gravel pit…forgot to put on bug spray…Brindie rolled in a large, old, dead, very smelly and rotten fish; two baths later and she still reeks and is still tied up to the front door; thank goodness for the fresh breeze.*"

August 6, 2004; Jennifer, Amanda, dogs Flip, Brindie, Jasper, Lucky – "*Two girls, four dogs!…We arrived Friday night around 7pm after fighting I75 traffic. Yuck. Had spaghetti, corn on the cob, garlic bread for dinner…Took a walk down to the dam and watched a beautiful sunset.*"

Friday Sept 9, 2005; Crickie – "*Arrived at cabin at 4pm…The cabin looked great inside; it's always great to walk in and 'feel the love' and all the fun memories…took a bike ride down to the river; beautiful and peaceful… came back and cooked dinner and went out to look at stars…Saturday AM had breakfast outside on porch…Then at sunset I went swimming in River…*

ZEN OF ME

Journal entry: June 27-29, 1997
Jennifer

"It's Jennifer up here by myself for the first time with my beautiful dog Lucky...went running this morning and saw three wild turkeys and two deer...I couldn't have asked for more beautiful weather...last night got here just in time to go to the gravel pit for sunset. Splendid, as always.

Saturday... will probably spend most of the day outdoors enjoying the weather...

Sunday Lucky and I sat on the beach for awhile – a perfect day! Went back to Oscoda for frozen yogurt and a stroll through town. Got back very tired from all the walking and sun, laid down to rest for a while. Went down to the gravel pit for sunset again..."

I am by nature a fairly happy, optimistic person. The personal disappointments and pain of divorce can drag even the cheeriest among us down, and that is the unfortunate situation in which I found myself in the late summer of 1997. Mine was a marriage that was foolhardy from the start, full of naive hopes and expectations. Naive as it may have been, when it ended, the fear, anger, and hurt that I felt were devastating.

I did my best that summer to cope as I made daily revelations and discoveries of the unfortunate past three years. I relied heavily on family and friends (long, tearful conversations and midnight phone calls) to get me through each long day, and yearned for the day when it would all be officially behind me.

That "official" day finally did come, and it was with a sigh of relief and a feeling of rebirth that I now started my mornings. Little by little, I was recovering.

"Why don't you take some time off and go up north?" my good friend Jeff asked me about a month after my divorce was final. "You could probably use a little time alone to think and just get away from things."

I looked at him in surprise. My first strong reaction was "no way... are you crazy?" First of all, I'd never been up north by myself before; I'd always gone up there with a friend or family. It was a tiny cabin in the middle of the woods with no one around...was that really a good idea in my present state of mind? Secondly, did I really want to run off to a place where my now ex-husband and I had spent our second night together as a married couple? The idea seemed completely wrong to me, so I dismissed it almost before the final words had left Jeff's mouth. Mentally and emotionally, and certainly without realizing it, I was deep down in a post-divorce rut.

The rest of the week I trudged on emotionally, struggling to find that inner peace I was used to and so enjoyed. Work especially had become fearfully tedious. That Friday afternoon at the office seemed to drag on and on; I was plagued by unanswered questions and I had to fight off threatening depression. Jeff's suggestion suddenly came back to me, and an image of me taking long walks in the sunny woods with my dog Lucky, breathing in the crisp air of northern Michigan and tossing all of my cares to the wind flashed through my mind. Maybe being up north alone wasn't such a bad idea after all. It was then I made up my mind to go next weekend, to the place I'd spent so much time as a little girl, and typed an email to my boss asking him for next Friday off.

The time off was readily granted, and even though it was only one day off, I was grateful (it was the height of our busy season) and relieved to be getting away. To be honest, there was a bit of apprehension too, mixed in with the good feelings. It was true; I'd never been up north by myself before. I'd never had to turn the electricity and water on myself before, never had to deal with any problems with the old stove or water heater on my own. There was no phone up there, few neighbors; I would be completely cut off from any familiar conversation. I was used to being up north with friends and enjoying the laughter and gaiety of a roomful of people. Would I get up to the cabin and feel the emptiness and solitude close in around me? Would I want to turn around and head straight back home to the comforting arms of friends and family? In spite of my misgivings, I knew I had to try it.

"Come on, Lucky!" I called to my Husky/Collie mix that following Friday morning. She jumped up happily in the seat next to me in my little green truck. I had stocked up on a few groceries, and had also brought along the required books, sweats, a movie, dog food, my camera and my hiking shoes. Had I remembered my cabin key? I triple-checked my wallet for my cabin key and, putting my truck in reverse, Lucky and I were soon backing out of my driveway and heading up north.

My nervousness transformed itself into excitement as I pulled onto scenic River Road; I was about ten minutes away from the cabin. Lucky's snowy-white muzzle had been thrust out of her passenger window almost the entire drive, and she had been whining anxiously for the past hour.

"Here we are, girlie!" I said as we pulled up on to the cabin lawn. I opened the door for her and brushed off the seat she'd been sitting on. She bounded out of the car and raced around the cabin, then made a quick detour into the forest after a chipmunk, her favorite thing to chase. I found my key and walked up the cabin steps for the first time by myself. I took a deep breath and walked inside...cold, dark, quiet. I hesitated. I pushed on and walked to the little utility closet and fumbled to find the circuits; lights buzzed to life as I switched both circuits to "on". The refrigerator began to hum and the water heater gurgled, both welcome and familiar sounds to me. I let out my breath. The first thing I did was to go around to each green-paned window and pull back the heavy checked curtains, letting in the afternoon sun from all sides. What a world of difference it made to have the sun streaming in every window, warming the old tiled floor and setting off patterns and shadows of leaves on the familiar overstuffed chairs and couches. Lucky came bounding up to the front porch, breathing hard and already muddy from her first romp in the forest. She had a big smile on her face as I let her inside and she ran over to gulp down half a bowl of water I'd set down. I finished unloading my things and did the first thing I usually do upon arriving up north - got out my big wool slippers and curled up in my grandfather's old rocking chair with my book.

Lucky cut my reading time short that afternoon, demanding a walk in the woods; she didn't come all this way, and have the unexplored forest all around her, to sit on the rug and watch me read. I tossed the fuzzy hair on her head and dug out my hiking shoes. We let the screen door slam as we walked down the bumpy lane, through the big white gate and out towards the river. I unleashed her and kept my eye on her as we walked; no real need for worry though. She was such a good dog that she'd stay with me, never getting too far ahead, deep in the woods to my left or right. I watched her trot along, jumping over logs, freezing at the sound of a chipmunk, then dashing off in an eternally vain attempt to catch it. The fun was always in the chase for her.

The sun warmed me as we took a high path along the river bluff, and I stopped to sit and just look at the river for a while. Lucky raced down the bluff and lapped up the clear water below. The wind blew my hair across my face and I smiled, realizing that for the first time in months and months, I had not been thinking about lawyers or in-laws, ex-husbands or accusations. I looked down at my legs in jean shorts dangling over the bluff, and then out at the far banks of the winding, gentle river and felt something inside that I'd lost, and hadn't even known I'd lost: hope. It came back to me in a small dose that afternoon by the river, watching Lucky play around in the water below with the balmy air blowing across me, breathing in the sandy smells of the river that I'd known since I could remember.

We walked back to the cabin that late afternoon and grilled hamburgers outside on an open fire for dinner. I had to admit that I felt a little nervous about nightfall; "night" up north is a world of difference than "night" back home. There are no city lights, no sounds save for animal sounds, deep in the forest. The night up there is midnight thick; a twig snaps and it is heard echoing on and on through the darkness. I shrugged off those feelings and pulled on my favorite pajamas, turning on one of the dim lamps next to the rocking chair for some bedtime reading. As I sank deeper and deeper into my book, I forgot about my aloneness. Lucky's soft breathing and the gentle rocking of my chair in the silence lulled me off to a near sleep. Jerking up, I knew I should get into bed. I let Lucky out one last time and shuffled off to my bottom bunk, cushioned with a fluffy comforter and heavy pillow. Lucky hopped up onto the bed and I was asleep before I knew it, my first night alone up north turning out to be a completely non-momentous occasion.

That next bright morning I felt refreshed and better than I'd felt in quite a long time...too long. The cabin was cheery and already the breeze was warm and bringing with it smells of the Huron forest. I made a pot of coffee, extra strong, and yawning, let Lucky outside. I wondered what time it was, and turned to grab my watch from the antique dresser in the bedroom. Something made me stop as I walked across the room towards the bedroom, and an idea came to me, something I'd never done before: I decided then to spend that whole day with no time. I wanted to float through this day which dawned cloudless and warm, letting the world drift by as I felt, but did not know how fast, the day was passing. I needed a day when I did not know or care about time ticking by. I turned my watch over without looking at it and made sure any other clocks or watches were similarly tipped. The moment I turned my watch over, I felt another something I hadn't felt in many months: freedom.

The cabin is one of the few places I know of where the passage of time simply does not matter. There are no lawns to mow, no phone calls to make, no TV shows to watch, no deadlines to meet. I sat at one end of the big green wooden oval kitchen table that morning, sipping my coffee and reading my book by the light of the early morning sun. It was going to be warm, I could tell. There was not a cloud in the sky as I looked down at Lucky and thought about what we could do that day, our timeless day.

Unfortunately, the divorce and all the struggles and emotions that go along with it had turned me into a temporary pessimist. I thought about taking a drive that morning, through some of the neighboring towns, but wondered really what of interest there was to see. I thought about heading east to Oscoda and the beaches of Lake Huron, but I looked at Lucky's long thick hair and thought the hot sun without shade would be too much for her. I began to feel defeated before I'd even started, and felt a twinge of old depression coming on, the first I'd felt since I'd gotten up here yesterday afternoon. I pushed those thoughts aside and promptly decided to take the drive to the lake that morning and to the nearby town in the afternoon. Determined not to let myself be weighted down by any negative thoughts, I finished my toast and brushed the crumbs off the green and white-checked tablecloth; I had started to win the battle. As I quickly washed my few breakfast dishes, I felt hope and happiness return as I reminded myself that I had no idea what time it was.

Getting ready to go any place, once you're up north, takes about thirty seconds; there is no primping or fuss. You just grab your car keys and purse and head out the door. After I finished my coffee and juice that morning, I pulled my hair back in a ponytail, slipped on my flip-flops and called to Lucky to get going. She jumped happily in the front seat with me, her usual spot. I rolled down the windows and headed out into the day.

It took me about 20 minutes to get to Lake Huron that morning. Lucky and I pulled up into a roadside park and found a path leading through the woods and to the beach. I had brought a blanket, but no book. I just wanted to think for a while, and who knows; maybe I wouldn't think at all? I looked for a spot in the shade so Lucky wouldn't get too hot, but there was little shade near the water. We found a spot hidden by tall sand grass, away from the few other beach-goers, and I spread out the blanket and sank down gratefully in the soft sand and warm sun. Lucky took her cue from me and, facing the water and the breeze, stretched out next to me. I dug my heels in the sand and ran my fingers through it too. The wind tossed my hair as the sound of the waves crashing onto shore lulled me to close my eyes as I sat there. The occasional squawk of a seagull broke the warm silence, or the yell of a child down the strip of beach, building a sandcastle. The minutes passed by as I felt myself drifting away, loving the peace and quiet of the late morning.

I had no idea how much time had passed before I suddenly remembered Lucky sitting quietly next to me, and that I was supposed to be taking care that she didn't get too hot. I looked down at her and she was fine...happy as a dog could be, sitting there on a blanket on the beach, staring at the seagulls and, nose in the air, sorting out all the scents that drifted her way on the lake breeze. My fingers kept slowly sifting through the sand, and I buried my feet and ankles for variety's sake.

Lucky had stretched out next to me and was sleeping when I thought we should head on to our afternoon drive to any neighboring town to look around; those little towns up north can be quaint, charming and pleasantly surprising. Lifting my head up into the sun once more, I realized I didn't want to leave my newfound breezy haven. Peace had been a long time coming for me, and once I found it, I was unwilling to give it up. Smiling into the sun, I remembered my hesitation at coming to the beach and softly shook my head; somewhere inside, a lesson had been re-learned... confidence was returning. I stood up, Lucky jumped up too, and we walked down to the water's edge so she could take a drink and play for a minute, and I could get my feet wet. Draping the sandy red and black-checked blanket over my shoulders, the two of us walked slowly back to the car, warm and sleepy from the morning at the beach.

Instead of driving directly on to the afternoon's foray, I thought ice cream was a necessity at that point. I drove to the Dairy Queen on the corner for a chocolate-vanilla twist soft serve, large, and got Lucky the kiddie size in vanilla. We sat together at the sticky plastic tables, me trying to lick my ice cream faster than the sun could melt it, and feed Lucky hers at the same time. Both of us ended up with ice cream in our hair; laughing, I had to go back to the window for extra napkins.

I had noticed upon driving into town that there was a lakeside art festival going on, with crafters selling their wares from temporary booths down by the lake. Knowing I had time, I gently tugged Lucky in the direction of the lake again, and we browsed through the little booths selling nature photographs, homemade jewelry, yard ornaments, embroidered sweaters, and native pottery. People stopped to pet Lucky and tell me what a pretty dog she was; I found myself smiling at people and wanting to chat, something I hadn't felt like doing in a very long time. The day stretched out before me, warm and welcoming. We left the homey, friendly art fair and walked back up to the Dairy Queen parking lot where I had left my little green truck.

Lucky and I hopped back into our respective seats, and I pulled out a map of Oscoda and its environs. I had no idea where I would head; I thought I would just look at the map and find something interesting and head there. This little map I was looking at had all the usual county and town roads, bridges and streams, but also had local places of interest marked, which for up north means places like historical libraries, scenic overlooks, and fish hatcheries. With my index finger I perused the old black and white map that was ripped at the creases, waiting for something to grab me. Suddenly I found it; a small town near a lake called Sand Lake, on the outskirts of which I found the map marker: "pioneer cemetery";

seemed much better than a fish hatchery. I folded the map open to the section of the county I needed, put the truck in first and Lucky and I pulled out of the parking lot, heading south.

The day was warming up, and I had the windows rolled all the way down. We cruised along the two-lane highway, ignoring the speed limit signs somewhat and enjoying the forest on both sides of us. Occasionally another car would zip by us, but we almost had the roads and the forest to ourselves that day.

The slower speed limit signs were my clue that Lucky and I were getting close to the town and the intriguing pioneer cemetery. We first came to Sand Lake, which is a large, beautiful, glassy lake, surrounded by adorable summer cottages with screened in porches and willow trees, complete with tire swings and sloping grassy back yards. Every cabin had a rickety wood dock extending out into the smooth lake, with a pontoon or fishing boat, or even Jet Ski bobbing next to it. Kids with inflatable swimmies on their upper arms ran off the edge of the docks, holding their noses and doing cannon balls into the water. A few of the cabins had picnic tables in the back yards, with barbeque grills already smoking with afternoon hot dogs and steaks. The lake had come upon me suddenly, and I didn't get to take it all in and enjoy it like I would have liked. After seeing how inviting it was, I drove all the way around it once, then drove around it again, more slowly this time, for a second look; I smiled and relaxed, knowing I most certainly had the time that day for another drive around this serene little lake.

Watching the miles click by on the odometer, I knew we should be getting close to where the cemetery should be. Suddenly up ahead in the road I noticed a backup of cars; on these nearly empty roads, this backup seemed out of place. As we got closer I got my answer; I had pulled up behind a funeral procession. I slowed down to their speed, and kept a respectable distance behind; today of all days I had the time to drive behind and wait.

I followed this slow moving line of cars all the way to the cemetery; the pioneer cemetery. They all pulled in to complete the final stage of the funeral for the loved one they would all miss, and I pulled off on the side of the road across from the cemetery. I just wanted a quick look and hopped out of my car and trotted across the street; at the risk of seeming like I was gawking, I still wanted to see the cemetery and read the dark green

Michigan Historical Marker at the entrance. Lucky yelped in vigorous protest as I left her behind in the truck with the windows cracked.

For such a sad, quiet place, this wooded final resting place was peaceful and beautiful. The headstones were of simple stone, the flowers abundant and natural. The forest closed in tightly, hugging the outer rim of the farthest markers. A bright, crisp American flag flapped slowly in the gentle air. It was a quiet, whispering type of afternoon, nature adding to the somber air of the event taking place before me. The funeral procession had stopped and people dressed in black gripping tissues began to climb out. I walked up to the historical marker in my flip-flops and began to read. I learned that the land for this plot had been purchased in 1870, and early stagecoaches on the Tawas-Manistee stage line passed by this very spot on their homesteading journey. Reading on, I learned that the marker recognized not only the cemetery and the old dusty highway, but also the countless unmarked graves of those early settlers. My eyes drifted up to the well-dressed men and women in mourning, climbing out of their sleek black limousines and freshly washed cars; what a difference a century makes. I took one last glance at the funeral still in progress, and turned and ran back across the cracked road in my jean shorts and t-shirt, thankful that I could walk away from this funeral as simply an uninvited observer.

Late afternoon began to have hints of dusk and Lucky and I said good-bye to beautiful Sand Lake; I was dreaming unrealistically of yet a second vacation home up north to come to. My stomach began to growl as I consulted my old map once again, getting us on the right road back to the cabin. I made an impromptu swerve in to a mom and pop grocery store and bought a homemade beef pasty (a Northern Michigan specialty too good to pass up when authentic), gravy, coleslaw and a Diet Coke for dinner, putting the greasy paper bag out of Lucky's reach as I jumped back into the car. The day had been wonderful, and seemed to stretch on for much longer than a normal day. There had been no official beginning to it, and with no watch on my wrist, I could feel no official end to it. I made the rest of the drive back to the cabin in happy, reflective silence.

The sun was beginning to set, breaking bright orange beams into the cabin and across the green wooden table as I sat there in silence reading my book and eating my pasty. I fed Lucky a few flakes of crust and put my dishes in the sink. Stopping at the window to look outside at the sunset, my mind drifted back to this morning, when I'd stood there and had so many doubts about the day ahead of me. I thought about what I'd done that day: an uneventful trip to a beach I'd been to countless times before; a visit to a sticky Dairy Queen; an unexpected stop at a small-town art fair; a discovery of a serene lake and cabin retreat; an unpretentious historical marker pounded into the ground. It had been a simple day, full of simple, easy things. Why then, did I feel so alive and excited on the inside, like I hadn't felt in many months? It had more to do with my outlook on my day, my timeless day, and not so much with the things I saw or did. It was the return of hope, confidence and strength.

Looking back on that day now, I can see that I had finally glimpsed life outside the rut again, and gotten a taste of how good fresh air can be.

Because the sun had finally set and darkness was settling in, and not because it was "time", I changed into my summer pjs that night and curled up in the rocking chair with my book. The crickets had started to sing and Lucky was already stretched out in front of me fast asleep as I began to read. I couldn't concentrate on my book; my thoughts wandered instead back to my friend's suggestion two weeks ago that I come up to the cabin by myself, for some needed "think time". Reflecting, I couldn't help but remember how negative and doubtful I'd been about this whole trip from the start. I'd been negative about coming up here by myself, about taking Lucky to the beach without shade, about finding anything interesting in a tiny town among tiny towns. Now here I sat, legs stretched out in front of me in my favorite chair, feeling like I'd seen the world today. Where would I be right now, if I hadn't decided to come up here? Images of me, watching a movie by myself in my living room, or sitting at my parents' house going over bad memories with them...it made me shudder. I leaned my head back on that familiar thick headrest and looked up at the beloved sagging ceiling of the cabin, listening to the trees outside rustling in the night air. I knew I could not have gotten out of that rut had I stayed home this weekend. A black and white cracking, crooked photograph of my grandma and grandpa Hale sitting at their kitchen table, their heads bent together and smiling, looked down on me, in my grandpa's chair. Their little cabin they unpretentiously built so many years ago offered me hope, relief, freedom, and escape; it gave me life. This was a day I dozed off at a beach, ate ice cream with a dog, drove twice around a lake, swerved off the side of a road to read a roadside marker, and made a split decision to have pasties for dinner. I had started to be excited about life again. This one simple day in the sun changed the way I was living my life, in so many small subtle ways. I closed my book, which woke Lucky up and off we shuffled into the back bedroom. I crawled into that handmade bunk and was asleep before my head hit the pillow.

Next morning a balmy breeze streamed through the cabin windows; another hot cloudless day. Today could not be a day like yesterday though, and the minute I picked up my facedown watch from the dresser, reality returned. I sighed as I noticed that I had awakened later than usual; time was ticking away. Stretching and yawning, I pushed my feet into slippers and let Lucky outside to chase the first chipmunks of the day. As I made the coffee and heated up some oatmeal, I knew I had time for one long walk along the river that morning, before I had to come back and start cleaning and packing, and driving back. I knew not every day could be a day like yesterday, so perfect and revealing. That was fine with me, though. I had learned what I needed to yesterday; now it was time to head back home.

After our walk along the river, I cleaned up that afternoon at a leisurely pace, clinging to my cabin attitude for as long as I could. When the cabin was spic and span again, I closed the last curtain and locked the last window shut. Driving back down the road away from the cabin, I shed the usual few tears and said good-bye as I looked at Goodnufrus in my rearview mirror. And as usual, I consoled myself with the knowledge that the cabin would be here for me again, the next time I needed it.

****

Weeks later I was back into my normal routine of work, workout, take Lucky for a walk, read, sleep. My good friend Jeff, who had suggested I go up north over the summer, had invited me out for a drink that night. He and I sat at the bar of an electric nightclub, ignoring the throbbing music and trying to carry on a conversation. I sipped a beer and he a mixed drink, and he asked me how my weekend up north at the cabin was.

"Mmmmm..." I murmured, remembering the peace. "It was absolutely wonderful. Just what I needed. Thanks for the suggestion that I go and get away."

He smiled at me. "And how are you feeling and doing now? How are things going for you?"

"MUCH better. You know, as each day goes by, things get a little better and the past slips away a little more. I don't think about it as much as I used to."

He took a sip of his drink. "What did you do up north?"

I set my beer down and told him about the walks along the river bluff, the grilled dinner, the morning at the beach, the giant softserve cone, the cozy little art fair, the drive around Sand Lake, Pioneer Cemetery, the huge beef pasty, the raging orange sunset. Then I told him about my timeless day on Saturday, how, on a whim, I spent the whole day simply drifting along with no watch or clock.

He laughed a little and said, "You know, that's very Zen of you".

I finished a gulp of beer and looked at him blankly. "What is?"

"It's a very Zen thing to do, a Zen concept, that concept of timelessness, of no boundaries, of nothing to mark a beginning or end to a day, to life lived."

"Really?" I asked, smiling at him.

Who knew? I knew nothing about the teachings of that ancient way of Eastern thought. I only knew that I'd had one day up at the cabin that I would always remember, for its beauty that seemed to stretch on forever, and for the way I came back, peaceful and ready to start living my life again. I also knew that for me, there is one place on earth to find that unique kind of peace, in a little cabin that my grandparents built so many years ago.

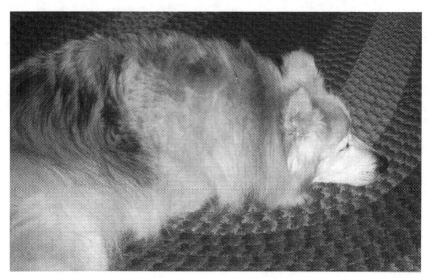

Lucky at the cabin, 2005

CHAPTER THREE

The One That Got Away

From the Journal…

July 27-28, 1981; Gennie, Brian, Trisha (friends) – "*For the short time we were here, we got lost in the woods two times. Then we went to the dam. Came back and did nothing. It rained! On the back porch there is a bat under the wastebasket!*"

May 23, 1987; Shirley or Annie – "*…arrived Sat 2:30 pm. Both pumps working quickly. Cold in the cabin…oil stove on all weekend! Weather mostly gloomy with short periods of sunshine…Forest fires didn't come close enough to evacuate as the winds did not shift. Firemen patrolling the area – <u>all this 1 week ago</u>. Steve and MaryAnn arrive at 1am…Ann & Shirley arrive 4:00 pm. Crickie & Pat arrive 4:30pm Sunday. All sang 'America the Beautiful' and 'The Gang's All Here'…not really.*"

Saturday July 16, 1988; Annie & friends – "*Annie and Patti went fishing below the dam…Patti's sister Ellen, her friend Mike and his son Mikie, along with Karen and her friend Karen, all sat down for a fish feast…*"

May 22-23, 1990; Matthew & Bobby – "*We arrived at 5pm, and being the rugged, outdoorsmen, we both promptly took a nap…Emily & Lloyd told us about a 450 lb bear they had seen in the area…Few people were around since it was the middle of the week. The same could not be said for the mosquitoes, unfortunately*".

May 21, 1992; Steve, MaryAnn, friends, dog Chance, Bill, Pat, Crickie, Shirley, Annie, Don, Bobby, Chris Cowles and more dogs Molly, Stanley & Lowie – "*We had to buy a new stove. Found a used appliance store & had stove delivered…Thursday BIG STORM, from Alpena to Flint, Houghton Lake & between. Trees & poles down. Cooke Dam & this area escaped any damage… Five or Six tornadoes confirmed. Much much damage to eastern Michigan… Also made our usual trip to Ben Franklin's for new sweats, shoes, etc.*"

August 25, 1992; Crickie – "Arrived at 1:30 pm after spending the weekend at Janie & Walt's for the 4th annual Hale Family reunion...Janie sent me off with fresh 'home-grown' eggs, honey, some delicious green pears, bread and leftover snacks...Headed north in search of a gas station. Traveled many miles on empty before finally filling up...Went for a delightful swim... First night went to bed early. Woke up to the sound of wings fluttering. Had the feeling something had just flown past my head...Turned the light on...could hear wings flapping and something banging against screen...noise continued...squeaking, little finger nails on the screen...on-no! There it was! A creepy crawly brown furry BAT!! AAAArrrrgh! HELP! Oh there's only me...Donned my Tawas Bay elite Cabin Club jacket...old wool socks on my hands...unhooked screen. Held my breath...hit screen with stick many times before bat finally dropped off..."

September 22, 2004; Don & Bobby – "Fixed light above the kitchen table...Walked from one end of Oscoda to the other, took plenty of pictures, had ice cream cones in Oscoda, talked to the neighbors, walked in the woods, sat on the river bank, saw flock of wild turkeys, one deer, circling hawks, ducks and a couple of beavers...no clouds in the sky...talked to fishermen...rented John Wayne videos."

September 11, 2006; Don & Bobby – "From Don Berkemeier. I like things that are old, but still look nice and work. Hence, we have a new 1954 Johnson outboard motor...(11 steps on how to start the motor follow)...12. It's a good idea to take the oars also."

THE BEAR CLUB

JOURNAL ENTRY
   OCTOBER 6-13, 2001
   Jennifer

"Jen arrives around 1:30 and heats up the cabin. I went to the grocery store for water and snacks and sweets. Kris, Doug & Arlene arrived around 6:00 pm..."

"The next day we rode the Queen...cheap beer, rickety folding chairs, bad P.A. system, out of hot tea, very bad jokes, beautiful scenery – just as I remember it."

"It snowed Sunday...we took blankets & lots of sweatshirts for our Queen ride."

"Monday AM. I went jogging and it was 20 degrees out...Arlene made Aunt Ruby's buttermilk pancakes for breakfast..."

"...we went for a walk and played hours of euchre and drank hot chocolate..."

"My guests left around 2:00 pm on Friday – so quiet after they left – a little lonely too. It has rained all day. Am going to go into town & get a pizza for dinner."

As much as I love going up north to the cabin by myself or with my sister (my usual cabin companion), there are times when I invite a few friends to liven things up and share in the experience of Goodnufrus.

"Turn left onto the dirt road called Chipmunk Trail, drive through the white gate (it looks locked but it never is) and you'll see a beautiful white cabin on the right with a paved driveway, mowed lawn and fresh paint. Keep driving..."

Such were the directions I emailed to pals Doug and Arlene, and an old traveling companion Kris. These three old friends of mine were to be my adventure mates up at the cabin one week in early October. Like most young people I know, they were used to working long and hard hours at their jobs in downtown Chicago, and they jumped at the chance to spend a week in northern Michigan in the crisp clear air with nothing more to do than catch up on sleep, drink coffee, take walks in the woods, and eat good food.

I met Kris in college through some good friends. Kris and I discovered our mutual love of Taco Bell and good beer, and the rest is history. We rarely spent a day apart through our remaining three years in college together, finding many more things in common than a penchant for fast food and sipping imported beer. Kris and I discovered within each other a similar love of travel and discovery. As our graduation day neared, we spent many a night at outdoor cafés drinking espressos and talking for hours about going to Australia to see that great wild continent. We would part company at the end of the night excited and hopeful, but never sure if our crazy plan could work. Then one night we decided to make it happen and we put our heads together.

After graduation we both moved home to Mom and Dad's and lived rent free, working hard for a year to save enough money to take our fantasy trip to the South Pacific. When we landed on the island of Fiji in 1990 was when I realized our dream was coming true. Thirteen weeks later my parents picked us up at a cold airport in Detroit, tanned, tattooed, hair bleached blond from the tropical sun, with "Fiji", "New Zealand", "Australia", and "Tahiti" stamped in the pages of our bright blue passports.

Since that incredible journey, Kris and I have added Germany, England, and Puerto Rico to the roster of trips we have taken together. We travel extremely well together; both like to get up early and get moving, neither likes to spend much time in front of a mirror in the morning, both like to meet the natives and both love to sample the local flavor in every way. It is always a joy to have Kris along for the ride.

Doug and Arlene are Kris' incomparable friends from high school. A wonderful example of what a marriage should be, they are so close and so a part of each other that it's almost hard to tell where one ends and the other begins. Between the two of them, they possess more brains than most ten people combined, accompanied by sharp wit, cunning humor, and an enviable lust for life. They live life to the fullest; traveling with them is like adding a fistful of lemon zest to the pot. We all share a love of getting off the beaten path and living new adventures.

Kris had been up to the cabin once or twice before, back in our college days, and loved it. I knew Doug and Arlene would delight in the old log cabin with the deer trophy, the slightly sagging roof, the tiny closet turned into a bathroom, and the giant old creaky bunk beds. I had just one small, nagging concern in the back of my mind; what could they possibly experience up here that they hadn't already seen or done? I knew that they had traveled around the world, had friends in many countries and had sampled so many of life's great varieties from cuisine, to sights, sounds, people, and natural wonders. Their apartment in Chicago was impeccably decorated with stunning black and white and color photos of caves, waterfalls, rainforests, and natural rock formations from around the globe. What things new and exciting could I possibly show them in Oscoda?

Kris, Doug and Arlene pulled up on the grassy front lawn of the cabin on a cold October afternoon. Folding my printed directions I had emailed to them and sticking them in the glove box, Doug extracted his six foot four frame from the tiny rental car they'd driven up there, one limb at a time. Kris and Arlene bounded out and stretched, throwing their heads back and taking in huge deep breaths of cabin air, devoid of even a molecule of pollutant of any sort. They were a long way from Chicago.

I had estimated their arrival time down to the minute; I had been cooking a big pot of chili for the better part of the afternoon. The cabin smelled like spicy beefy tomatoes and warm, dark pumpernickel bread, welcoming them to the cozy, friendly room, heated by the trusty old oil-burning stove in the corner. They brought their things in (flannels, hiking shoes, a huge cooler, scarves, t-shirts, bottles of wine, groceries, reading books, cameras and binoculars) and once they'd each picked a bunk bed, we settled in to an early dinner, tearing off huge chunks of the steamy dark bread and dipping it in our chili. With full stomachs and sheepskin-lined moccasins donned, we settled in to the big stuffed rocking chairs and talked over the week that lay ahead, planning for adventures that really can't be planned at all.

I woke up first the next morning and padded out into the chilly cabin, turning up the heat on the little stove. The sun was just coming up as I pulled my bathrobe close around me and made my way sleepily over to the old coffee maker to get a full pot of Fog Lifter brewing. I pulled back the thick gingham curtain to let some morning sunlight in and got quite a surprise: an early northern snowfall, thick and heavy!

You just never know, with Michigan; in years past I have been up north in early October and have spent the entire week in shorts, tanning myself on the riverbank in 80-degree weather. Kris, Doug, and Arlene are fortunately all hardy Midwesterners, and had packed for every possible weather scenario.

I went lazily around the cabin as the strong-smelling coffee started brewing, and pulled back all of the green and white-checked handmade curtains. The welcoming smell of the coffee brewing brought my three friends out of their deep slumber and I heard them start to roll around in their bunks, yawning. Doug was the first to come dragging out of the bedroom, rubbing his eyes. He stood there in the middle of the cabin, staring at the snow outside. Heavy, still-lingering sleep and disbelief made him stare out the window for a while, speechless. Then, "Oh, geez..." he finally said.

It really was a beautiful, if completely unexpected snowfall. The flakes were thick and heavy, and made the surrounding evergreens all look like Christmas trees. The sun cut sharply through the snow, sending its orange rays slicing through the falling snow and causing the newly white ground to sparkle. We sipped our coffee and each curled up in a favorite overstuffed chair to wake up and catch up with each other's lives. Soon we were laughing, listening to Mozart, and licking the goo off our fingers from the warm, sweet homemade pastries I'd bought from the German bakery in town and warmed in the oven that morning. We spent an entirely relaxing couple of luxurious hours in this way, talking, eating, sipping, laughing, and stretching.

It wasn't long before I'd brought up the exciting fact that the neighbors in the white cabin had been having nightly visitors in the form of two large black bears that had been raiding their birdfeeders at night. At first, our neighbors had been alarmed, but gradually they'd gotten to the point that they were filling the feeders daily, not only for the birds but also to sit on their porch and watch the bears come and, lying on their backs, dump the seed into their open mouths. I was excited because, with all the talk of having black bears up near the cabin, in my 35 years of going up there, I'd never seen one. I had been hoping to see one each time I'd been up there; no luck so far. My friends' eyes lit up at the talk of the big, wild creatures roaming so close to the cabin.

"We'd LOVE to see one too; we've never seen one in the wild, either". We all agreed it would be a real thrill and we'd all keep our eyes open.

Two empty coffee pots later, the talk turned to the plans for the day. We didn't let the fact that it was snowing and cold outside alter the plans that we'd made last night for our first day together up north. In spite of the weather, we were determined still to ride the Queen.

The Au Sable River Queen is a large, brightly painted (in red, white, and blue), double-decker paddle-wheel boat that has cruised up and down the beautiful Au Sable loaded with tourists, for as long as I can remember. It sits docked near a campsite about 15 minutes from our cabin. For a nominal fee you get a two-hour boat cruise on the open-air vessel that smacks of Huck Finn and Tom Sawyer. You get to filter through the world's most amazing gift shop, where you can buy t-shirts with girls in bikinis fishing on them, moccasins, Native American drums, and polished river rocks. Hot chocolate, weak coffee, hot dogs, beer, pop and potato chips are all available on board from rusty folding tables, sold by local volunteers. Your cruise is narrated by a would-be comedian, who is unaware of how ineffective the loudspeaker system is on the Queen. The narration comes across in much the same way as the muffled teacher on Charlie Brown; occasionally, words come across clearly, and amidst the gobble you'll hear "fall colors", "Native Americans", "trappers", "hundreds of years ago". Go up top and you'll find the air thick with smoke and people sitting at a makeshift bar, drinking beer and even occasionally glancing at the passing river scenery.

As small-town as is this lovely water-borne piece of Americana, there may be no better way to experience the beauty of the Au Sable, especially if you can catch a cruise during the first few weeks in October, when the Fall colors are in full swing along the river banks. You begin to question the authenticity of the paddle wheel however, as you hear the engine sputter to life a few minutes before you push away from shore.

My parents bought me an Au Sable River Queen t-shirt when I was about 5 years old, and I wore that shirt until I was 12 and it was too small and tight for me to even put on. I hated finally getting rid of that shirt! For old time's sake, I recently bought myself a new Queen t-shirt, this one in large, so I'm sure not to outgrow it this time.

That snowy morning, we tossed aside the shorts and t-shirts we all packed with great optimism, and donned instead our long underwear and flannels, stuffing our ear muffs and warm mittens in our winter coat pockets. We barely managed to squeeze all the Polartec and goosedown inside the economy rental car; a few minutes later and the little car was backing away from the cabin, slow and stuffed full, like a pampered fat cat.

Fortunately, it is just a short ride from the cabin to where the River Queen departs from the shore. We rolled out of the car and trotted towards the gift shop like kids to a candy counter. Soon, we girls were trying on Native American necklaces and Doug was eyeing himself in a corner mirror with a coonskin cap sitting askew on his head. With one eyebrow raised, he asked us what we thought of the hat. We gleefully gave him the thumbs up, in the hopes that he'd buy it. I ended up buying some "homemade" fudge and Doug reluctantly put the cap back as the bell sounded for "all-aboard".

We shuffled aboard the Queen; it was a good thing we bought our tickets in advance because the boat was full for that tour. The snow had mercifully stopped, but there was still a biting wind that nipped our cheeks and ears. We picked two benches in front of each other, right in the middle of the boat, on the lower deck. I immediately went up to the gray-haired man in camouflage selling the hot chocolate and got myself a big Styrofoam cupful. Soon, others were standing in line behind me, doing the same thing. And beer. People were getting beer too, at 11:00 am. It wasn't long before the guy in hunter's orange operating the keg was the busiest guy on board. Before the boat even shoved away from shore, I saw several people in line for the second time at the keg.

The Queen pulled away from the shore and the paddle wheels started spinning. We were heading down the river, clutching our hot chocolate, grinning at each other and eating popcorn. The day had started to warm up a little as the sun rose further in the bright blue sky. The fall colors were just beginning to hit their peak, and the sun lit the tips of the trees on fire, heightening the already vivid reds, oranges, golds, and burgundies. We strained our ears to catch even a piece of the running narrative on board; the rigged-up speakers in the corners of the boat crackled and sputtered. Soon we stopped trying to understand the muffled speech and just sat gazing at the river and the forest as we slowly chugged on.

As the boat turned around to make its return cruise up the river, I was returning to my seat with my second cup of hot chocolate.

"Where are Doug and Arlene?" I asked Kris.

"They wanted to check out the upper deck", she said.

Fifteen minutes later and Doug and Arlene hadn't come down yet. I nudged Kris. "Wanna go up and see what they're doing?"

She was game so we carefully made our way through the crowd and up the broad wooden stairs to the second deck.

It was like walking into another world. Downstairs was the G-rated deck, the calm, serene, peaceful family deck, the deck for scenery watchers and photographers. The upper deck was the Bacchanalian deck, the rowdy deck, the deck for parents after all the kids are in bed. Even though the upper deck was completely open, there was a thick cloud of cigarette smoke that hung over it and traveled with it up the river. There was classic rock playing from an old boombox on a chair in the corner; there was a mini keg up here so that people didn't have to make the journey down to the placid deck below for a refill. People were playing cards, laughing, shouting, and doing anything but looking at the river slowly ambling by. Big-shouldered men with thick hair and beards, in Carhartts and hunting boots, leaned back on rickety old folding chairs and told loud jokes over the music. We found Doug and Arlene wedged in between an old hunter telling stories and two middle-aged housewives, trying to escape from men at home. The gray-haired storyteller had found a listening ear in Doug, who had developed a rapport with the keg guy, and an understanding that his plastic cup was to be filled when there was about one sip of beer left in it. Arlene was making fast friends with the two home-weary housewives, lending her sympathy and robust support of their domestic plight.

Kris and I stood there, giggling at the scene. We waved and managed to catch Doug's eye. He grinned back at us joyfully, saluting us with his plastic beer cup; the old man didn't notice that Doug had turned away, and kept on talking. Kris and I decided that a few minutes on the upper deck was enough for us. The smoke and the slow rocking of the boat were making me a little heady. We waved bye to Doug who was getting his cup filled again, and gingerly made our way back down to serenity.

Kris and I were able to get our seats back and spent the rest of the boat cruise in contented silence, watching the water lap onto the colored shoreline.

We had a tough time prying Doug and Arlene away from their newfound friends from the upper deck of the River Queen. We did manage to drag them away, and all of us piled back in the little car, laughing at the morning's events. Arlene confided that she had half-promised to meet the two housewives up at the saloon that night, but confessed that she'd really rather stay home with us that night and make her much requested corn chowder. We were glad that she did, as it was a treat. Thick, hot, and a little spicy, it was the perfect end to a wonderful day spent on the river, making new friends, seeing new sights, reading a few chapters in a favorite book, and reviving old memories.

The next few mornings began much the same as our first morning had, minus the snow. Fortunately, the weather cooperated for the rest of the week, not snowing anymore but still remaining on the chilly side. Whoever was up first in the morning would get the coffee going and turn up the stove. We'd pull out the pastry du jour, a wide variety thanks to the German bakery in town, and pass it around for everyone to try. Our bodies got used to the shock of the extra heavy doses of caffeine in the morning as we'd make the coffee stronger and stronger, and linger over a few extra sips.

After breakfast, we'd pull on our jeans and sweatshirts, wrap scarves around our necks, hang binoculars and make sure our cameras were loaded. We'd head out the door for our first walk of the day, and get to the end of the cabin road and make a decision: turn left or right? Either way and we'd have hours and miles of walks ahead of us. Both directions took us along the spectacular Au Sable, winding its way towards Lake Huron. We'd turn right and head down the old campground road; after about 3 miles we'd start to see State campgrounds, chosen as campsites for their vistas overlooking the river. Each campsite had a fire pit built and a small area cleared to park a car and pitch a tent. There were 6 campsites built back along the river, in the deepest part of the forest, each one about ¼ mile apart. We made a game of choosing our favorite campsite, except it was impossible to choose a favorite. They all had such breathtaking views of the winding river; here a lone pine sticking up on an island; there a beaver dam fording the river; there a splash of trees so vivid we all pulled out our cameras to attempt to capture the beauty. All the way back to the cabin we'd argue the pros and cons of campsite #1 vs. #4, and so on.

Turn left at the cabin road and we'd be heading down towards the gravel pit and miles of trails that, unlike the campground trails which are high atop the river bluff, lead you right up to river's edge, level with the slow-moving water. These trails too wind through the very thick forest, with open areas created by State campsites. There are many great places to stop and sit down, and in the summertime, dangle your feet in the water. I have seen beaver playing in the water on these trails, and one summer had a river otter taunt my dog mercilessly for 20 minutes from 15 feet out in the water until Lucky finally slipped in frustration and fell in the river.

The four of us got to know those trails very well over the next couple of days. We took many pictures of ourselves against a backdrop of mighty evergreens, stark white birches, and painted maples. We took nature shots of rising dunes, twisted trees along the river, wild turkeys, and the sun glinting on the river at high noon. We'd return to the warm, welcoming cabin and off would come the hiking boots and on come the warm fuzzy slippers and sweats. Someone would get out the leftovers from the night before: grilled eggplant, pasta primavera, spinach salad, penne pasta with peanut sauce, or shepherd's pie, and we'd finish that off and drift off to a chair, books in hand. It wouldn't be long before we'd be dozing off or starting a crossword puzzle or a game of solitaire. After everyone had rested from the morning walk and hearty lunch, off we'd go again for the afternoon walk in the late afternoon sunlight. Nights were filled with music, good food, laughter, and Black Forest Chocolate Cherry Bugaboo ice cream. We'd break out the beer and wine and laugh long into the silent, dark night, playing euchre and creating new jokes to tell and memories to relive.

The first few days of our week up north together, we'd been fortunate enough to have beautiful weather…a little on the chilly side but lots of sunshine. The fourth day dawned with a loud thunderclap, followed by lightning and torrents of rain. We started our day the usual way – a couple pots of strong coffee and pleasant conversation. We skipped the pastries that morning and instead made homemade 7-up Pancakes, following a recipe written by my grandmother on a torn aging piece of envelope and still thumb tacked into the old cupboard door. The rain continued to beat down and I glanced discreetly up at the slightly sagging roof with just a little trepidation.

A few hours passed and the weather continued to be gloomy and stormy. The time came when we'd normally start to do the breakfast dishes and put on our old jeans and get ready for the first walk of the day. We had to quickly find a Plan B though, as Mother Nature was throwing a wrench into any plans for hiking that morning.

I began to run down in my head the things we could do up at the cabin that did not involve being outside. We could go into town and go bowling. We could go into town and go to the antique stores and tourist shops. We could go see a movie, we could…

"Yahtzee!" Someone shouted.

"Yeah, yeah!" The suggestion got quick approval from my guests. Apparently this game was one of their favorite rainy afternoon pastimes back in Chicago. I had played the game once or twice only so I was only barely familiar with it. Well, if it was good enough for them, it was good enough for me!

We got out the board and the dice, gathered around the giant old wooden kitchen table and wrote out our scorecards. Someone wandered over to the pile of cds we'd brought and put some music on. It wasn't long before the beer and wine were introduced to the table. We remembered the giant bin of salty hard pretzels I'd brought and had not touched until then. Soon a gloomy afternoon had been turned into a lively gaming party; we'd jump from funky R&B to salsa (which included impromptu meringue dancing) to hip hop and then some reggae. The Yahtzee got pretty competitive and the laughing louder as the afternoon wore on. By the time we threw out the last roll of the dice, the "never-ending" supply of hard pretzels was nearly gone, there were a few empty beer and wine bottles in the sink, and we'd all honed our Yahtzee playing skills considerably. We were having so much fun that we didn't notice the clouds breaking up; we did however notice when the sun finally broke through in the late afternoon.

A cheer went up around the table. We made a quick dinner and then broke out of the cabin and into the wet sunshine. The woods were dripping and the birds singing. We felt free...and we'd only been trapped inside since morning. We took a quick walk down to the river which steams after it rains, and got some beautiful photos of the muted colors from the turning leaves through the mist.

One of my favorite things to do up north is to make s'mores. It's not hard to convince people to have s'mores for dessert. We faced a little challenge though in trying to find dry wood to start a fire, so we cheated and grilled our s'mores over the old rusty barbeque grill. After my third s'more, the chocolate was pumping through my veins and even though I knew I would be grossly over-extending myself, I asked my guests if anyone would think horribly of me if I assembled my fourth toasty treat. No one minded in the least. Somehow, I figured as much.

We went to bed that night full from too much beer and s'mores. We kept the windows open and fell asleep breathing in that fresh rain smell from the surrounding pines. We'd faced our first day of bad weather and made it through beautifully.

Our last full day together dawned bright and sunny. The anticipation of the plans we'd made brought everyone from the big soft bunk beds out into the living room a little earlier than usual. We made our pots of coffee but instead of lingering over the steaming cups we washed up and got dressed for our road trip. We had decided to drive north up the east coast of Michigan and on to the top of the Lower Peninsula, peruse the multitude of tourist shops at Mackinac City, then take the Mackinac Bridge over into the Upper Peninsula and have lunch. We'd enjoy a leisurely day gazing at the fall scenery, buy some tacky souvenirs, and drive back down the middle of Michigan on small roads through small towns back to the cabin, to complete the up north experience.

Within an hour of waking up, we had done the morning dishes, spruced ourselves up (as much as one can without a shower), picked out the road trip cds and were cramming ourselves into the trusty and by now tired rental car. We bumped our way down the cabin road and onto the smooth paved straightaway, headed due east towards Oscoda and the scenic coastal road.

The day was perfect; blue skies, slightly warmer, not a cloud in sight. With Guns n Roses blaring from tiny speakers, we zoomed along the near empty byway. We made our first stop a few miles north of Oscoda at a family-owned gas station and party store, buying Pringles, pop, and Cheetos. Road-tripping college students had nothing on us as we shouted and waved at people we didn't know and careened out of the parking lot.

We became silent as the expanse of Lake Huron came into view to our right. It is breathtaking, stretching as far as the eye can see. The deep blue of the cold white-capped water, the sun glinting off the waves, mirrored the blue of the sky. Seagulls bobbed up and down with the rhythm of the great lake. Couples held hands and held onto their floppy hats as they walked the beach together, keeping an eye on their bounding dogs ahead. Pieces of driftwood dried in the sun, long strings of seaweed clinging and dripping from the roots.

We continued our drive north, resisting the urge to stop at every inviting antique store or quaint fudge house. A few hours later we started seeing signs for the Mackinac Bridge, and it wasn't long before we were pulling into the parking lot at one end of a long string of the state's best tourist shops. Dusting the Pringle crumbs from our fronts, we pushed our way out of the rental car. Fudge shops, wool shops, dollar stores, woodworking shops, puzzle and kite stores, local artist shops, and t-shirt shacks awaited us.

We spent a couple of hours wandering in and out of the alluring stores, chewing on fudge and trying on huge winter woolen coats. Collecting our new trinkets, we made our way back to the car and on to the Mackinac Bridge.

No matter how many times I cross this windy, five mile long bridge, it's still a thrill to see the barges and sailboats, Mackinac and Drummond Islands, hundreds of noisy diving seagulls, and the wooded and rugged shoreline ahead of the Upper Peninsula. We found a beautiful place to eat in St. Ignace, designed to look like an old train depot and sitting right on the rocky shoreline overlooking a rough Lake Michigan. By the end of the lunch, the waitress was our new best friend and we shouted our good-byes to her as we boxed up our leftover burgers and salmon dinners. The sun was just beginning its afternoon descent as we rumbled back over the bridge and zipped past the tourist shops of Mackinac City.

Driving back down the forested middle of Michigan makes a nice contrast to the drive on the beautiful shoreline and views of Lake Huron from the east coast. We had the road and the brightly turning forests nearly to ourselves as we headed south back to the cabin. The first half of the trip back was spent on a major highway; as we turned off I75 heading east on to a smaller, two lane byway, the terrain became hilly, and the colored woods more dense. Farms and quaint houses with large front porches and beautiful wildflower gardens dotted the hills. Horses and cows grazed together, flicking the flies rhythmically off their backs with their tails. Hawks circled lazily above in the late afternoon sky.

We were 30 minutes away from the cabin when Kris leaned forward from the back seat and said urgently, "Uh, you guys? I *think* I just saw a black bear in the ditch by the side of the road back there."

We turned to her, roused from our dreamy sightseeing to stare at her. "Really??"

"Hey Doug", I said. "You feel like turning around and going back and checking it out??"

His answer was to slam on the breaks, turn the little car around and step on the gas again, heading back to the spot in the road where Kris directed us.

We were almost back to the spot when, about 35 feet in front of us, a huge black bear lumbered its way up from the ditch and into the road ahead of us. It shuffled its massive frame slowly across the road, its eyes on the hill in front of it. No one breathed in the car as we watched this amazing and elusive animal make its unhurried way to the other side of the road. The afternoon sun glinted off its shiny black coat as, massive shoulder muscles rippling, it broke into a slow, mechanical lope going up the grassy hill on the other side of the road; it went over the hill into the sunset and out of our sight.

There was complete silence in the car for about 5 seconds, then we broke into a uniform excited scream. We'd all finally seen our first black bear, together, and what a sight it was! We were on top of the world. After the hooting and hollering and high-fiving died down inside the car, we quickly formed the exclusive Bear Club, and made a top-secret handshake for members only.

We turned the car back around and continued heading home towards the cabin; we couldn't stop talking about the bear.

The early evening sky was painted in streaks of bright orange, flashing over the tops of the trees and lighting up the gentle grassy hills, to this day one of the most spectacular sunsets I have seen anywhere. The breathtaking sunset was a fitting ending to a day of friends and enchantment.

The next morning Kris, Doug and Arlene sadly packed up their
long johns and hiking boots, wiped down their empty coolers,
and gathered their books and decks of cards from around the
cabin. We shared one last big breakfast together and one more
strong pot of coffee. After many robust hugs and promises
to write soon, I watched them bounce down the rutted dirt
road towards civilization. The cabin seemed quiet and empty
without them there. I picked up my book but felt restless and
put it down again. I looked around the cabin and shifted my
feet. I took the journal from off the wall and grabbed a pen.
I began writing. "We saw a bear!!..."

Au Sable River Queen

CHAPTER FOUR
Remember When

From the Journal...

July 18, 1981; Don, Bobby, Matthew, Amanda, Geoff, Heather – "Today we all put on life-preservers except Mom and jumped into the water below the dam...there was a nice current and we drifted downriver. We then climbed a dune and were rewarded with a great view of the river...At night we all went over to the point and had roasted hot dogs and three fish. Geoff and I spent the night in a tent there."

August 23, 1982; John, Leslie, Kevin, Kristen – "It is my first trip back here since I was pregnant with Kevin and it's great to be back! The kids fit right in...Grandma Shirley being the veteran woodsperson and very excellent cook has caused us to gain great amounts of weight in short periods of time... caught several pan fish the next day. Kevin is a great caster and Kristen has discovered the marvel of worms!...We went to Alpena Tuesday to see the Dinosaur Zoo...We stopped at the Paul Bunyan site also (John and I were there on our honeymoon)...We love you Grandma Shirley!"

September 3, 1993; Steve, Crickie, MaryAnn, Nancy, and dog Chance – "It was Steve's birthday so we celebrated with hotdogs on the grill and chocolate birthday cake...Labor Day MaryAnn, Nancy & Crick got up early, left cabin at 6:30 am to drive to Mackinaw City so we could walk across the Bridge. We did it! Rode a school bus across to St. Ignace then walked back across with thousands of other people...beautiful weather...windy on the bridge...We had a great time. Stopped around Mackinaw City, saw the bagpipers marching through the town, then drove back to the cabin."

September 29, 2000; Shirley – "My hands are so cold I can hardly write! I'm here to meet with a furnace man who hopefully will have answers... Furnace man came, says we really need more oil."

August 5, 2005; Matthew, Kristen, Lauren, Don, Bobby, Jennifer, Amanda, dogs – "I came up Friday with my two daughters...hadn't been up for over ten years...It was great to see all the old wicker furniture, as I remember racing toy cars along the arms when I was a little boy...I was a bit disappointed to find that the old siren on the wall no longer worked...Jennifer and Amanda brought too much junk food...how can anyone resist cookie dough? We took a walk down Jennie Street and talked to a nice man named Wayne Small...his father used to hunt up here and knew Cliff Hale well. He had some good stories about the 'old days'...

November 4, 2005; Erik Lundeen (Jessica Wood's husband), son Max, friends Mike, kids Mackenzie and Clayton – "Unbelievably warm and beautiful day. Took the kids down to Gary's dock and watched sunset and threw rocks into the water...rode scooters down big hill in lower parking lot (FUN!) Hot dogs and tater tots for dinner...NOV 5...Played football, soccer, and flew kites out front in Gary's field. Went to Lumberman's and walked the steps, played in the sand dunes..."

June 22, 2006; Don and Bobby, Amanda's dogs – "This will be 'no-frills' weekend as I forgot bedding...Don just crawled in between a flannel sheet already on the bed and a couple wonderful quilts...tomorrow we hope to go canoeing below the dam...So many things up here to fix; Friday taking boat to repair place...Saturday in Oscoda had lunch at the firehouse, went to Arts & Crafts show on the beach, then to Red, White, & Blue Collar Festival at Wurtsmith Air Force Base...Sunday took the canoe to the gravel pit, paddled down to the dam, tied up at the fence...walked up the memorable hill just like we did SO many years ago to buy an ice cream from Mr. Delmonege who had a little store across from the well where we used to get water...

July 23, 2006; Annie and friend Evie – "Happy birthday Annie!...we ate breakfast then went for a nice walk to the dam, stopping several times to enjoy the view and Annie told me some of her memories. We decided to walk back through the woods by the river...We drove into Tawas for some shopping and were not disappointed...Went back to the cabin and grilled steak and veggies on the grill…TUES…had breakfast and now have to think of leaving to return to reality – ugh."

September 2, 2006; Don & Bobby – "…Friday we drove to Hale and drove into a camp that I thought was to be Camp Moqua. Found out it was Camp Mongotasee, the boys camp across from Moqua; Janie and I went to Moqua for 2 summers so we have some good memories…it's where I first learned to swim! The lodge has been bought and turned into a home…also saw the boat house and the remaining huts, but these are all new rustic homes on the lake now…they said we could tour the camp, which we did."

THE BIG LAKE GITCHE GUMEE

JOURNAL ENTRY
OCTOBER 4-11, 2003
Jennifer, Amanda
Lucky, Jasper, Brindie

"Time for Mandy and my annual trip to the cabin for the fall color changes. We got here early Saturday evening to a very chilly cabin…made some nice hot chili…Next morning frost on the roads; good thing for hot coffee! Monday morning woke up and went for a chilly morning jog…loaded up Manda's truck for the trip to Munising in the U.P. …a pretty packed car (3 dogs and two girls)…6 hours later we rolled into Munising…not a cloud in the sky and warming up to 70 degrees…Munising is quaint and lovely…sitting right on Lake Superior…town is 4 square blocks…The shipwreck tour is fabulous! For 2 hours we tooled around Munising Harbor…gazed at the southern Superior shoreline, Pictured Rocks, dazzling fall colors…saw 3 shipwrecks through the bottom of the glass-bottom boat…2 of the ships were built in the 1800's …the detail that can be seen is amazing…had full views of portholes, broken masts, giant metal bolts…cruised by an old lighthouse built in the mid-1800's used to guide ships into the harbor. That night we feasted on Muldoon's pasties, and had homemade fudge for dessert. Can you get more "U.P." than that??"

The legend lives on from the Chippewa on down
Of the big lake they call Gitche Gumee
Superior, they say, never gives up her dead
When the gales of November come early.

I was ten years old when Gordon Lightfoot wrote "The Wreck of the Edmund Fitzgerald". In 1976, his song was played over and over across the airwaves as it rose up the charts. The popular song goes on to tell the true story of a tragic shipwreck where all lives were lost in a violent but not uncommon storm on Lake Superior. On the Big Lake when it's Man vs. Lake, the lake will almost always win. The song captured my imagination even as a young girl and I had most of the words memorized; "Does anyone know where the love of God goes?" indeed.

The foreboding scene of a violent and deadly shipwreck was easy to imagine, even for me at a young age. I always pictured Lake Superior as the wild one of the Great Lakes, cold, rough and with giant waves crashing relentlessly on the shore. As a young adult I had never been there and so this lake always remained a mystery to me, subject to the whims of my imagination.

It's been a long time since I've heard "The Wreck of the Edmund Fitzgerald" on the radio; every now and then the classic rock station plays it. Something about that great lake has always tugged at my sense of adventure; the lake itself, the shipwrecks and the tragic lore that go along with it. It was a combination of restlessness and spontaneity that finally got me driving up the center of Michigan and across the Upper Peninsula to Lake Gitche Gumee.

It was June of 2003 and my mind was already drifting ahead to my October vacation, when my sister Manda and I would be heading up north for our yearly fall color week at the cabin. I sat there on my lunch hour one day at work, surfing the internet, trying to find a new and creative side trip for us to take; a mini-vacation within our vacation. Quite a few sites caught my eye, describing hikes through the wilderness in Michigan's Upper Peninsula, bike trips, waterfalls, sailboat trips. I suddenly sat up straight as my eyes caught the words "shipwreck tours on Lake Superior".

I was hooked; the words excited me. I stared at photos of bobbing cruisers in the bay at Munising Harbor, cruising the deep rough waters, at the bottom of which rest an unknown number of historical shipwrecks. The site went on to describe the Lake Superior shipwreck tour at Pictured Rocks National Lakeshore, aboard a glass-bottomed boat. My imagination took me to the north shore of the Upper Peninsula, to the rough waves and the rugged coast. I pitched the idea to my sister and she too was thrilled. I began making calls that day to the local hotels in Munising to find the ones that would take dogs; I called the shipwreck tour company to get prices and schedule a tour. The more I researched this beautiful and alluring town, the more thrilled I was to go. After I booked the tour and we'd chosen our hotel, it was a struggle to just sit back and wait while I ticked the days off my calendar.

Being busy at work made the summer months go by quickly. The third week in October came at last and Manda and I were comparing grocery lists and tying up loose ends at the office before we signed off the computers for a week.

Manda met me at my house early on a chilly Saturday morning, the day of our departure. We drove out of our suburban neighborhoods, both of our SUVs loaded to the gills with groceries, dog food, books, flannel, cameras, binoculars, videos and dogs.

The three hour drive up north was fairly typical that day; the dogs getting settled in the back seat, the phone calls between my sister and I ("did you remember the hot chocolate?"), and the deepening color change of the trees as we drove further north. We pulled up to the cabin in late afternoon, with plenty of time before evening to get the cabin warmed up, get the dogs settled down, and start dinner cooking on the stove. The dogs raced around and around the cabin, chasing each other, thrilled to be up north again; it's an escape for them too.

Unloading our trunks and depositing our bags in our respective rooms, we made the usual comments about how clear the air was and how good it smelled out in the woods. We each picked out our bunk beds for the week and dug out our warm woolen slippers, which we needed right away against the evening chill. Manda and I spent the rest of Saturday night making the cabin our own, setting out washcloths and face cream, and hanging up jackets. We had the week's menu and activities planned out by the time we pulled our hair back and curled up under the big featherticks for the night.

The trip up to Munising and the shipwrecks was scheduled for Monday, so we had Sunday to relax and unwind, to slowly unravel and let the fact that we didn't have to hear an alarm clock for the next seven mornings sink in. We spent the morning breathing in the crisp clean northern Michigan air while taking our favorite walks, and throwing sticks into the steel blue Au Sable for the dogs to fetch, ignore, or bring back to the bank to chew on. It was a mutual decision to have no agenda or timetable for that first day.

Back at the cabin that afternoon, we took inventory and decided we were low on essential groceries such as gourmet coffee, fruit pastries from the German bakery in town, and big loaves of homemade bread from the local market. This realization had us hopping into one car and promptly heading into town. We were hoping that our visit to downtown Oscoda that day would coincide with Paul Bunyan Days again (I had stumbled on this priceless local festival one year), when all the local men drive around in their trucks dressed like the famous logger: big beards, flannels, boots and overalls. But no, apparently we missed the quirky holiday that year, but still saw lots of men in flannel and beards nonetheless.

Having made all the required stops in town, (the dollar store, the German bakery, and Glen's Market - they have the best selection of ice cream), we headed back to the cabin, which was now almost too warm thanks to the tiny but powerful little square stove in the corner. That night we grilled hamburgers stuffed with onions outside on the grill, then cleaned it off and roasted s'mores. Full and sleepy, we covered up the grill, cleaned up the kitchen, and let the dogs out one more time before curling up under our Hudson Bays in the soft bunk beds for the night.

Next morning was the day we were leaving for Munising and the U.P. The day dawned warmer, and without a cloud in the bright blue sky. We had booked our shipwreck tour for the following day, so we had no reason to hurry that morning; it was a five-hour drive up to the U.P. and we had all day to get there. Seeing as we'd each had one too many s'mores the night before, we decided to take a jog down by the river before the morning wore on too much.

The river in the chill morning air is breathtaking; the quiet mist rises from the water and hangs over the river, hazy, quiet and serene. The tiny lone fishing boat bobbing in the middle of the river looked like an eerie ghost ship as we slowly jogged by. The three dogs raced on ahead of us, exploring the water's edge and splashing in the river. We jogged an extra mile, thinking ahead to the pastries warming in the oven, then turned back to the cabin for some badly needed coffee and a quick bird bath over the bathroom sink.

Refreshed from the morning jog, strong coffee, and nine hours of sleep, we were ready for the trip to Munising. We threw a few overnight things in one car, loaded up the dogs, closed up the cabin and started on our northward way. We had decided to take a lesser but much more scenic route, US 23, to get to our destination, rather than the main and more direct route up the center of the state, I75. By taking this route, we had a breezy lake bluff view of Lake Huron on our right for the first half of the trip. With its whitecaps, seagulls, driftwood, seaweed and endless horizon, the lake offered its usual stunning views that can lull one off to a peaceful retrospective silence. By early afternoon we had broken out the cheese and crackers and diet Cokes; as the day wore on, it kept getting warmer and warmer until we finally found ourselves in t-shirts and jeans with the windows rolled down.

"Can you *believe* this???" I asked Manda as we tossed our heavy coats and flannels in the back seat. This 80 degree weather was very unseasonably warm for northern Michigan in mid-October; we considered ourselves very fortunate and reveled in having the best of both worlds: hot, balmy, breezy climate and the stunning, breathtaking northern fall colors all around us.

The soft, sandy beaches of Lower Michigan gradually gave way to rocky, craggy shorelines as we edged the car over Mackinac Bridge. Seagulls darted and dove around us as the wind buffeted our car and we pushed over the bridge. Mackinac and Drummond Islands beckoned off to our right; Mackinac with its history, horse-drawn carriages and gabled mansions with multi-storied verandahs, and Drummond with its wild ruggedness that spoke of bears, hawks, and wilderness. I made a mental note to come back to the area someday; but for now we drove on, looking at our map and knowing we needed to find Highway 2.

We discovered the drive along Highway 2, along the south shore of the U.P., was itself so scenic and beautiful that it alone was worth the drive we'd taken so far. The small highway hugs the rugged, rocky Lake Michigan shoreline, twisting past tiny beach summer cabins for rent, warm inviting sand dunes and old wooden convenience stores selling fish jerky and pasties. The sand from the beaches drifted across the two lane highway as we sped along in the afternoon sun, both of us dreaming of coming back someday to this beckoning shore for some lazy summer fun.

Being in the Upper Peninsula of Michigan is like being in another world. The towns are tiny and far-between; most consist of cabins for rent, a gas station, a garage, a tiny library and a mom and pop grocery store that specializes in the local fudge, smoked fish, cheese, jerky, jam, and pasty recipes. The scenery ranges from dense evergreen forests with undulating hills, to softly sloping beaches, to rivers cutting through the forests and bluffs overlooking rocky rough shorelines below. Manda and I enjoyed the views as we zipped along the narrow road, the afternoon turning into evening as we approached Munising.

We had made it there in good time, thankfully locating our hotel on the outskirts of town without any trouble.

The two star hotel we'd found welcomed dogs; we told them we had only one dog as we checked in at the front desk with Manda's small, happy American Eskimo named Jasper cheerfully wagging her tail, charming the hotel staff. We thought it would be wise to sneak my two dogs in the back entrance, my stocky and powerful Staffordshire Terrier lunging and staring wildly around her at the myriad foreign sights and sounds of the hotel. The hotel may have reversed their friendly policy of accepting dogs on the spot if they could have seen me being dragged down the hallway, suitcases falling off my shoulder, being pulled erratically towards our room by my nervous canine.

Suddenly the cozy cabin we'd just left seemed spacious as we entered our room and situated suitcases for two, three dogs, one large dog cage and other dog supplies into the smallish room. We were two tired adults, three excited dogs, one small hotel room, barking dogs next door; add one pizza with breadsticks, unsuspecting delivery guy, room service, and cookies from the vending machine; it had the awkward, humorous makings of a bona fide reality show.

We stayed in that night and opened the windows a crack, enjoying the warm evening breeze; every now and then we got a hint of fresh Lake Superior air drifting in the window. The hotel offered continental breakfast, but we agreed to skip the coffee, juice and bagels and see what more inviting things we could find to eat next morning in Munising.

Our dogs woke us up Tuesday morning as the sun broke over the lake.

"Do you want to shower first or should I?"

I told Manda to go ahead and I'd jump in after her. Having a hot shower while we were up north was a real treat for us; we both intended to take full advantage of this luxury while we were here.

Freshly showered, we took the three bouncing dogs out the back and into the adjoining suburb streets for a long morning walk. I couldn't wait to get them settled back in at the hotel so we could head into Munising to explore, and then on to the shipwreck tour; the excitement to be out on the harbor on that beautiful day was making me walk faster.

"What do you want to do in town?" Manda asked me.

"Mmmm, I'd love to find some coffee, and just wander around. Oh yes, and I really do need to get some motion sickness pills". Unfortunately, I'd been suffering from bouts of motion sickness on every bobbing boat and twisting, turning car on a mountain road since I was 16 years old. This time, I was going to be prepared for it.

"Sounds good to me!" Manda said as we gathered up our purses and gave the dogs fresh water, saying good-bye to them for the day. I glanced back into the room at our three curious and energetic dogs trying to push their way out with us. I'm not sure what was in Manda's mind, but I know I was sincerely hoping our hotel room would look at least somewhat similar when we got back that night to the way it did as we left.

We had given ourselves a couple of hours to explore Munising that morning, and we were absolutely charmed. This tiny town of about six square blocks sits nestled at the foot of some beautifully sloping forested foothills, with the forests closing in on 3 sides and Lake Superior crashing in on the north. The town is sleepy, friendly, welcoming and could easily be a movie backdrop for a film that required a berg with "old time charm". The only question was where to go first.

"Oooooh! Let's go in HERE" I said, grabbing my sister by the arm and pulling her into a little coffee and pastry shop, with an antique coffee grinder in the window, a bench out front on a brick patio, and one tiny unoccupied round table next to a big sunny picture window. We ordered cappuccinos and hot, crusty apple strudels right out of the oven from the owner, and sat down at the table to chat and eat our breakfast. Hot coffee, fresh pastries, views of Lake Superior through a quaint wooden window with peeling paint...beats continental breakfast in a hotel conference room any day of the week.

Finishing our apple treats, we took our cappuccinos to go and turned right outside the little shop. We wandered in and out of the antique shops, Das Gift Haus, art shops, a combination bookstore and ice cream parlor, and made the trip to the drugstore (for the motion sickness pills and postcards), snapping photos all the while. The day was another record-breaking warm one for the UP, with a cloudless blue sky and brisk lake breeze. I looked at my watch and noticed the time, getting a sudden image of what might be going on back at the office right then: co-workers struggling with a stubborn copier, computers crashing, deadlines looming and endless voicemail.

"Manda, we better head to the dock for the tour" was what I said, pushing thoughts of the office out of my head for good.

Warm and full from the coffee house breakfast, we drove the five minutes to the boat dock and our shipwreck tour. The office where the tours set off was an old lake house, dining room and bedrooms converted to a souvenir shop and a small office. A huge bay window overlooked rough, white-capped Lake Superior and the dock where our glass-bottomed boat was bobbing. I quickly took my motion sickness pills and browsed the gift shop, fingering books written by local authors about the shipwrecks, ghosts of drowned sailors, Lake Superior lore, and lighthouses. It was almost time for us to board the 50-foot touring boat and jet out to the harbor. I looked at my watch impatiently; I had been waiting since June for this trip. But then, if I thought about it, in reality I had been waiting for this trip since I was 10 years old.

Manda and I and about 25 other tourists gripped the outstretched arm of the captain as we boarded the bobbing tour cruiser. We all had extra coats and jackets over our arms, none of us knowing what kind of weather October and a rough windy Michigan harbor on an open boat would bring. I was prepared that day: winter coat, then flannel, then sweatshirt and t-shirt; I was determined to not be one of the cold passengers.

There were all types of smiling guests that day taking the tour, from gray-haired seniors to young couples with their families. We all filed on board, quickly trying to find our sea legs and gratefully locating a free spot on one of the long benches on both sides of the boat. Even though we were just sitting at the dock, the glass bottom of the boat attracted all of us immediately. Manda and I looked at each other and smiled with excitement as the boat shoved away from shore and turned its nose toward the expansive harbor of Munising. Through a spray of lake mist and an intense wind, we all listened as red-haired Captain Joe began his narrative about the history of the harbor; he had a captive audience. He told us about the shipping history in the area, about the shipwrecks all along the coast, and the Native Americans who once lived here, his love for his town evident in his speech.

Munising Harbor is home to at least three known shipwrecks, boats built in the 1700 and 1800s that went down in the often treacherous harbor while trying to find safety from the even more dangerous Lake Superior during stormy weather. These 150 foot long wooden ships of eras past are amazingly intact, and sit in about 20 feet of clear water. We cruised along out to the shipwreck sites, listening to our captain, skimming along the tops of the waves in the late sunny morning.

Fifteen minutes later we had reached our first shipwreck site; perfect timing - we were all at the peak of anticipation thanks to the stories from our captain. Our driver proved himself an expert as he positioned us over the first underwater wreck. He maneuvered the boat directly over one end of the sunken hulls, then cut the motor. All of us jumped up as the boat stopped and jockeyed for our own section of glass to peer through; the driver let the bobbing boat begin to drift slowly and quietly lengthwise over the dark wreck below. What we saw gripped us all - the water was amazingly clear and the first glimpse of that eerie, massive old prow beneath us made us gasp as one. We stood riveted to the glassy bottom of the boat as the dark wreck below slowly glided by. The watery treasure beneath us was so clear and sharp that we could see rusted nails in the planks of the ship and rivets in the portholes. We were mesmerized, breathless. This ship was so wide that we could not see all the way across, in spite of our vantage point from above. Three foot long fish swam lazily in and out of the ship's old portholes as we pressed our faces up to the glass. I felt like I could reach through the bottom of our boat and touch the dark, weathered wood of the sunken deck, where sailors once walked, swore, and worked. The day was warm but I got a chill as I thought of the captain and crew as their ship hit the sandbar and began to take on water in the night. Without the benefit of modern naval and communication technology, this ship from two hundred years ago didn't stand a chance. My mind shifted from the cries of the crew and their desperate struggle, to myself as a child, sprawled out on my bed, listening to a song about a shipwreck.

In about ten minutes we had drifted over the whole boat; we had been given a view of a sad history that not many people have seen. We saw the boat from prow to stern, had seen her deck, mast, and the holes in her side. As bravely as she and her crew had fought the violent storm, the icy lake, and the staggering winds, Lake Superior had proven too much for her.

Our driver broke the silence on board by turning the motor back on, and Captain Joe began telling us about the next wreck we were going to visit. The next two sites were as moving as the first, and all of us on board observed them in the same awed and respectful silence.

An hour passed and we had seen all three sites, all of which invoked powerful scenes of a tragic past. The second part of the tour was icing on the cake: a cruise up and down the Pictured Rocks shoreline, which is the best way to view this rugged northern coast of the Upper Peninsula. The Pictured Rocks are forested cliffs of stratified limestone rock, stretching for miles in both directions. This part of the lake offers very few beaches; instead the waves crash and spray on the jagged edges of the cliffs and boulders below.

Manda and I decided the best way to see this part of the tour would be from the observation deck up on top of our boat. We climbed the wooden stairs up, gripping the metal handrail as the boat tossed and heaved. The day had grown warm, and I shook my head in disbelief as I took off my coat and tied it around my waist. There was not a cloud in the sky as we sped along, the wind whipping my hair out behind me and the sun warming me. Manda stood next to me on top of the boat, taking in the majestic cliffs, the dark evergreen forests, and the choppy blue lake surrounding us. I looked over at my sister and smiled. As I looked out from the middle of the harbor back at the shoreline of Lake Superior, I realized I had made it. After twenty-five years of wondering what this great lake was like, I was now sitting in it and enjoying the views. I had seen the shipwrecks and heard the true stories; I had met the people and even sipped their coffee. The boat began its big, wide, arching turn back to the dock and it occurred to me that it wasn't such a silly thing after all, to chase down a childhood dream.

Back at the dock, Captain Joe offered us all his hand again to help us get safely back on solid ground. We hopped off the white-washed boat and everyone thanked him for the thrilling trip and zipped their cameras back into their bags. As we were filing off the dock, the Captain gave us one more bit of information, and that was that Muldoon's had the best pasties in town, and they were right down the road; he highly recommended we stop there for dinner. Manda and I had come to respect the Captain and so we took his advice, and made the stop at Muldoon's for beef and chicken pasties, hot from the oven. Heading back the way we came, we also made a quick veer into the Hen House for the required sweet treat while up north, homemade fudge. Dinner and dessert were in the bag.

"How do you think the dogs are doing?" Manda asked me as we started the car and pulled out of the Hen House parking lot. To be truthful, I had been trying not to think about that. I wondered how much the hotel would charge if my dogs chewed the legs off their tv stand.

"Um, well, I hope they're doing fine." It was too late now anyway, I felt, to avert any disasters. Looking at our watches, we realized we had a couple of hours or so to kill before the serious dinner hour was upon us, so we made a detour on the way back to the hotel to Miner's Falls and Miner's Castle. We hiked to misty, crashing Miner's Falls, which are best observed from a wooden overlook built at the end of a narrow path leading into the forest. The afternoon sun broke through the thick surrounding trees as we took pictures from the overlook, hoping our cameras didn't get too wet from the spray. Walking back away from the falls and continuing on the path, we now walked out of the woods and along the top of the high windy lake bluff, towards the next tourist hotspot. We hiked until we reached Miner's Castle, a wild and beautiful unique rock formation which juts high out over icy blue Lake Superior. From the lookout point at Miner's Castle we could look up and down the cragged shoreline at the striped, forested cliffs stretching as far as the eye can see; this part of the trail was truly a nature photographer's dream. Looking down we got a little dizzy from the height; the clear depth of the foaming water and the waves crashing on the rocky, rugged beaches below made us grip the guardrail a little tighter.

I stood looking out over the lake and my eyes drifted to Munising Harbor. To look at it from the shore, it would be impossible to know about the mysterious shipwrecks lodged forever below in the sandbars. Those shipwrecks are one of Lake Superior's little known secrets.

We spent that night in much the same way as the last, except this time instead of pizza and vending machine cookies, we had thick homemade pasties and mouth-watering deep chocolate fudge for dinner. The dogs crowded around us, begging for a tidbit but really there wasn't much left by the time we were done. We took the dogs for another walk out back in the parking lot, watched a little local tv, and turned in for the night, cracking our window again for the warm October air.

After lingering in the nice hot shower one last time before heading back to the cabin, Manda and I packed up our bags the next morning and while she checked us out of the hotel, I deftly snuck my dogs out the back door and into Manda's car. This time we took advantage of the hotel's coffee and juice and drove off sipping on both and munching on hard bagels. I turned to get a glimpse one more time of Munising and Lake Superior as we drove away; I made a promise to myself to come back and spend more than one day next time exploring the rough waters of the lake and the staggering beauty of the Pictured Rocks. I got out the map that was folded to the section of the U.P. we were driving through and, doing my part as navigator, made sure Manda knew which way to go to get us back on the road to our cabin.

The sun was just setting over the tops of the changing trees of the Huron Forest as we pulled up in front of the cabin that night. That small old cabin was a welcome sight. The dogs were jumping around in the back seat, eager to get out and run around and stretch their legs, and to put all memory of that tiny hotel room behind them. Manda and I got out of the car too and stretched our legs, unlocked the cabin and began to unload the car. "What do you want for dinner?" I asked my sister as she turned up the pot-bellied stove.

"How about some black bean soup?" she answered, which was great with me; it was one of our favorites. I went to the fridge and as we began getting dinner ready my mind wandered back to the day on the harbor and the shipwrecks, and I began to wonder if there were any other childhood dreams of mine that needed to be chased down and lived out.

Jennifer, Amanda and dogs

CHAPTER FIVE
Until We Meet Again

From the Journal

Sunday November 1, 1987; Annie & Shirley – "Arrived at 12:00pm to shut down the pump & drain the pipes…hate to have only a few hours here but spring will be here soon."

Nov 13, 1988; Annie & Shirley – "Arrived 1:45pm to shut down pump & water closet & to await the reupholstered chairs. Found out the lock on the door did not work. Had to break a pane of glass in the door to get in…"

Nov 5, 1989; Annie & Shirley – "Closed little cabin down – see you next spring."

October 1990; Bonnie (friend) – "Being on the river with Mary & Steve, the beauty of the river. Emily & Lloyd were <u>fun fun</u>…All in all it's something I will never forget. The 52 bombers are fast & loud; I like it. It's getting time for us to leave. Now it's crying time again."

October 25, 1991; signed MR (possibly Mary Roeder?) – "Life changes but not the Hale cabin. The walls hold many memories of the fun times I had, and will have. Thanks everyone for keeping it the same and for keeping it up."

October 21, 1993; Janie, Bobby, Pat, Shirley, Laura, Crickie, Annie, Mary, Carol – "Beautiful weather…walks, food, games, singing around campfire; one night 19 degrees, snug and warm inside…Can't wait till next year, same time, same place!"

October 24, 1995; Crickie & Shirley – "Crickie back up for a final, splendid fall color weekend. Walked at the dunes, saw a bald eagle soaring over the river...Shirley drove up early Tuesday to help shut down and close up our beloved cabin for the winter. Another season comes to a close."

October 31, 1997; Annie & Shirley – "Closed dear little cabin down & battened her up for the winter. <u>See you next spring</u>."

September 30, 2000; Jennifer – "...I am only delaying the inevitable. Does anyone else cry when they have to leave here? I start when I'm closing the curtains..."

August 23, 2002; Amanda, Jennifer, dogs Brindie, Jasper, Lucky – "We picked a bunch of wildflowers...I really hate to throw them out. Sigh, so sad to leave. This is what summer is all about. See you in October."

June 25, 2005; Don & Bobby – "Am really enjoying this visit – so many memories up here, the wonderful pine smell, quietness and peacefulness all around...Oh, it's beautiful up here; sure hate to leave as always."

November 4, 2005; Erik Lundeen (Jessica Wood's husband), son Max, friends Mike, Mackenzie, and Clayton – "...Leaving early to get home to get things done. Thanks Cabin! We had a great time!"

GOOD-BYE AGAIN

Every time I leave the cabin, I tell myself the same thing: "this time, I'm NOT going to cry". It's ridiculous, pointless, overly-sentimental. I've been to the cabin and driven away from it countless times. It's close enough so that within reason, whenever I want, I can drive up for a weekend or a week. What is it about those loving, faded, timbered four walls that grip me and don't want to let me go when it's time? The anticipation of the drive up north, the new book packed in your bag, the cookies you've been wanting to try, your dog curled up in the back seat. You walk into the cabin, open the windows or turn on the stove. It's deeply quiet. You shuffle around, humming to yourself, checking your watch to see if you have enough time for a walk to the river before dinner. Before you know it, the cabin has softly folded in around you; the big couches beg you to sink into them, the photos on the wall beckon another glance, the oven is ready for your hot apple pie. The warm breeze drifts in through the open windows, and you're excited and you don't know why. You have escaped to somewhere with no phone, no computers; old dishes, well water and a sagging ceiling, Outside is a deep blue sky, blinding white birch trees, endless acres of forest, a sparkling blue river and the softest sand dunes you'll ever climb. You have made your arrangements at home; someone will get the mail, do your work for you at the office, watch over your house. Up here, you are free. You are comfortable, warm; you have everything you need. You have peace, happiness and a quiet that stretches on and on. You will see deer, eagles, songbirds, jumping fish, spectacular sunrises and vivid sunsets; you will finish a book, eat too much and find your new favorite gourmet coffee. You settle in and immediately you are Up North.

That final day comes. Ugh. Time to pack up, fold up the shorts or flannels, shove everything back in your bag. Gather up the face cream, shampoo, hair clips, favorite snacks. You look out the windows, trying to remember the view and what the breeze feels like, so you can recall that when you're back home negotiating highways and trying to make it to work on time. As you clean, you try not to look at the couches, the old crooked photos on the wall, the half-eaten pastries still wrapped up in paper and sitting on the crowded cupboard. Everything gets methodically pushed aside, put away, and scrubbed down. The cabin is slowly letting you go.

It's clean now, the car is packed, you unplug the fuses and the place goes dark. Standing by the front door, the cabin is cold, quiet and sad. "Bye, cabin" is whispered into the dark room and you feel the response: "come back soon; I'll be here". The dog is already in the back seat, knowing she has fetched her last stick from the river for a while. She curls up, dirty and exhausted, ready for the long drive home. You jump into your car before you change your mind, start it up, and try not to look too long in the rear view mirror.

GOODNUFRUS is what you see.

I really do understand why I cry every time. If I'm feeling especially brave, I make a quick stop at the gravel pit for an official good-bye to that river I love. Then it's back in the car for good. Following the twisting river on that old, familiar gravelly road, I heave a big sigh and turn on my cell phone; getting ready for the entry back to civilization. The cell phone beeps on and I glance down at it; any calls while I was gone?

"SEARCHING", the phone reads on the front display. I smile. I like that. I like that it's searching.

Fifteen miles later I glance down again at the phone, and I frown to see that it now reads "EXTENDED SERVICE". I'm definitely on my way back.

Until next time.

Goodnufrus

FAVORITE SHORTS

It's the Simple Things

One day a few years back, I was sitting up north with my dad at the cabin, around the big green oval table. "Dad, how much do you think it might have cost back then to build this cabin?" We sat for a minute, looking around us at the simplicity and the materials used, and factored in the fact that a relative had done the physical labor. We came up with $1,000, back in 1945. Give or take a few hundred. Back then, and to the two couples involved, this was a good amount of money. I sometimes shake my head and wish my wonderful grandparents could see and understand the incredible (to use a current corporate buzz term) Return on Investment their half of their monetary input has earned. This little cabin, filled with hand-me-downs and chipped dishes, has become a place where love is born, friends are made, solace is found and lifetime adventures are had. Our family photo albums are not complete without photos of us as squinting kids, us as awkward teens and us as young sunburned adults with different cabin scenes in the background. In several families we are now on the fourth generation of cabin-goers.

The bluffs and beaches of Michigan are filled with cabins and second homes, some small and unassuming, some near-mansions with impressive landscaping and four-car garages. Big or small, we all use our cabins for the same things, to take our families and friends for long summer weekends to enjoy the water, sun, boats and the local ice cream parlors. Our kids play in the sand and ride their bikes up and down cracked gravel roads, the parents enjoy the open windows, the fresh air and the views, families together attend the local small-town festivals and holiday parades. In reality, it's the simple things in life we all enjoy, and it doesn't matter if your getaway is a little one-room log cabin or a multi-level work of art; it's about the people and hearts who fill those rooms and create the memories.

My Dad, the Smart Man

I will never forget the day when my parents finally decided us Berkemeier kids were old enough to take the little snowmobile out on our own up north. It was thrilling and a little scary at the same time. Often, back in the 1970s, we would go out riding through the forest and not see another human being for hours. We had spent so much time walking and exploring in the summers up there that finding trails was not a problem; the choice was simply "which one today?"

One late winter afternoon up north I sat waiting, snowsuit on, for my brother to return from his solo outing on the snowmobile; he seemed to be taking a long time. Finally, I heard the high-pitched whine of the Ski-Doo and jumped up to finish getting my warm winter gear on. My dad came out with me to put more gas in the machine, reminded me to not stay out too long and sent me zipping down the little cabin lane on my way.

I got to the end of the road and turned right, taking a short little drive down to the dam along the road. There were a few little bumps in the path, which sent me a modest foot or so in the air; for me, that was what it was all about. I started down the back road where I could really open it up and go fast for a while.

I looked at the sky and realized that unfortunately it would be getting dark before too long. I had been curious though, for a while, about this big hill in the other direction, and what was on the other side of it and what the view looked like from the top. I thought I had just enough time to ride over there and satisfy that curiosity.

I got to the bottom of the hill and gunned it; the old reliable snowmobile responded and up and up I went, and my heart started pounding a little faster. Yes, I was a little nervous, but this was the best. I got to the top of the hill and looked down at the frozen winter wonderland all around me. To the left I could just make out the icy Au Sable River, gray and foreboding. Spreading out in all directions was thick snow, peeling white birch trees and towering green pines. I stood still, taking it all in, my breath coming out in puffs. I turned off the engine, closed my eyes and listened; not a sound anywhere for miles and miles.

Minutes later and the setting sun urged me to get heading back to the cabin. Turning the engine back on, I tried to turn the snowmobile around, but the path was too narrow at the top of the hill to accommodate the wide arc that our snowmobile required to turn. As we often had to do, I got off and picked up the rear of the machine and lifted the end around. On the second lift, and when I had it almost turned around where I needed it, the trusty engine made a sputtering sound and then just stopped. Now complete and total silence again. I leaned forward and tried the starter, again and again; still nothing. Sun setting, miles from the cabin, me alone, getting dark, deep snow everywhere.

What do I do? I put my head in my hands and fended off a panic. If I could rely on my sense of direction, I calculated that if I walked down the big hill and off to the right, I would hopefully run into a small grouping of cabins known as Sid Town, which has some full-time residents but mostly is a tiny resort town that rents cabins and sells bait during the summer tourist and fishing season. Leaving the beloved machine behind, I swung my leg over the snowmobile and started walking.

I can't really say how far it was, maybe half a mile; to me, in the deep snow and dark woods, it seemed like hours. I finally saw and smelled the thin smoke from a fire coming from a chimney from one of the little cabins at Sid Town. Nervousness aside, I walked up to a strange cabin door and timidly knocked. I heard a chair being scraped as someone got up inside and slowly walked to the door. It was an older man, still in snow pants and smoking a pipe. In a very shy teenage voice I explained my situation, seriously wondering if and how this man could possibly help me. He grunted when I finished my story and shouted out to someone else in the house; from the kitchen came his son, who without hesitation donned his own snow suit, pulled on his hat and said "show me where you are"; off we went.

We found the snowmobile right where I'd left it. "Ah", said this young man, "you've got one of these old Ski-Doos." He tried the starter with the same result as I'd had an hour prior. He moved quickly to the back of the machine, to the padded back support that the last person on the seat always got to lean on. Poking his fingers down in the crack of the seat, he lifted up the cushions to reveal a little tool storage unit that I never even knew existed. Inside were various small mechanical tools, and a bundle of something wrapped in a nice soft cloth. The man took off his gloves and opened the small cloth quickly. "Hmmm. Cool" he said. He looked at me and smiled. "Your dad's a smart man" he said as he showed me the brand new spark plugs in his hand. He deftly moved to the front of the machine, lifted the hood and had the new plugs in their place in no time. I stood and watched in amazement as he jumped back on the machine and started up the snowmobile with no problem.

I am sure that smile on my face was unforgettable; I could not believe my good fortune. I asked my knight in shining armor if he wanted a ride back and he said no, he liked the walk outdoors. I watched him go as he trudged back to his little cabin and fire in the fireplace.

I climbed back on the snowmobile and slowly and carefully made my way down that big hill, my curiosity tamed for now. I zipped back to the cabin, turning on the big front headlight as it was now dusk and the sun had set. I turned off the machine at the cabin front door and walked inside, much to the relief of my parents who had indeed begun to worry. I walked directly to my dad and gave him a big hug and told him "thank you so much". My mom began helping me off with my wet clothes and I began to tell them my story and why I had been so late.

I of course never saw either man again, young or old. But I will always remember them as one part of my up north adventures.

The Hoot Owl

After my marriage ended in 1997, I found myself often doing things on my own. My sister and brother were married and busy; most of my friends were married or in relationships. It was during that time that I discovered and developed a love for being alone at times.

As many of us in our extended family have found, there can be nothing more soothing and therapeutic than loading up your car, taking your dog, making the beautiful drive up north and spending time alone at the cabin. It is truly a getaway for lost souls and sad hearts. It offers the polar opposite of working life in the city and suburbs, which we all yearn for from time to time. I had gotten into the habit of driving up north as often as I could, and if I couldn't find anyone to go with me, I'd go it alone.

One summer I was talking to a cousin at a family reunion. I mentioned I'd been going up north alone quite often, and truly enjoying it. She looked at me incredulously. "You go up there ALONE?" she asked me, her eyes widening. "You know there's no phone, no neighbors, right? What if something were to happen? You're kind of a sitting duck, you know." I laughed off her concern (motherhood had brought out her loving protective nature) and told her I actually loved the peace and quiet and being able to go and do what I pleased at any time.

However, I have to say, as assuredly as I told her I loved being alone at the cabin, her words stuck in my head as I packed a few weeks later for another solo trip up north. I engaged all of my inner bravado and confidence as I pushed her words out of my head and drove towards Oscoda.

Thankfully I arrived at the cabin during a bright and sunny afternoon. I got all of my things inside, got the dogs settled, and sank down into the big rocking chair in my flip flops and tank top to read. I rocked back and forth, enjoying the silence and the fresh air; how could this be scary at all?

Nighttime though is a different animal up north. And truthfully, there are no permanent neighbors anywhere close. Earlier than usual I put the little flimsy locks on the doors and found myself jumping at every twig snap and rustling of leaves. At last, I couldn't avoid it any longer;

time to go to bed and turn out the lights. I crawled into the lower bunk, curled up deeply under the big comforter and called both dogs up on to the bed with me. Pure, deep silence settled over the little bedroom and as the dogs fell asleep, I lay there with my eyes wide open.

And then I heard it; it was so close that it had to be right outside my bedroom window, in one of the pine trees within a few feet of the cabin: the low, soft sound of a hoot owl. I listened intently, still nervously frozen under the covers. It came again, right outside the window. And again, and again. So soft, quiet and reassuring. Slowly, I began to smile. And as I smiled, I could feel myself relax and my head sank into the pillow. Before too long, I was sound asleep in one of those famous cabin deep sleeps, not to wake up until the hot summer sun climbed over the pine trees the next morning.

The hoot owl serenade is something I have never experienced since then, but will never forget. That was a rare gift of God and nature. I have never again felt any fear about being alone up north, and continue to go solo at any opportunity.

The Moon and Cameras

When I am up north alone, I tend to only go into town for necessities and for a little sightseeing. When I am up north with friends, we take full advantage of the local eating and drinking establishments. That week with my friends Kris, Doug and Arlene was no exception. What started out with "let's go into town for souvenirs" quickly morphed into "let's go get a few pitchers and play pool at the Edelweiss". And so off we went. And we discovered that the Edelweiss has the best prices and best selection of imported beer in town, and a number of pool tables and dart boards as a bonus.

We four friends discovered many things that night. We found that after one pitcher of beer, none of us are good pool players. At two pitchers of beer, we're all very excellent pool players. At three pitchers, we are back to being miserable pool players. And so when pool soured on us, off we went to the Honky Tonk saloon next, for cans of beer and shots. We stayed for the treat of a can of Pabst and a shot of something, I don't know what. In spite of being obvious out-of-towners, the local regulars welcomed us and even begged us not to go when we announced we had a big day ahead the next day.

We piled in the car and began the twenty minute drive home, laughing and reliving the night. When we turned down Cooke Dam Road, the trees closed in around us and the night got even darker; we slowed the car to navigate the hairpin turns and narrow road. About a ¼ mile from the cabin we hit the straightaway, a quick last stretch of road that emerges from all the twists and turns that follow the river. As one, we noticed the big yellow, low-hanging full moon that seemed to be so close to the road that if we jumped, we could touch it. "Oh my gosh!" we said as one; we had never seen the man in the moon so clearly and so obviously looking at us. We swerved off the side of the road and jumped out, each of us with cameras in hand. Because we felt like the only ones in the universe, we lay down on the hood of the car and in the middle of the road, and stared into that full moon for quite some time. Finally, after many pictures and a desire to go to sleep, we made the rest of the drive to the cabin.

For the record, we also discovered that in spite of how many pictures you take and how good you think you are with a point and shoot camera, pictures of the moon on a dark night just do not turn out.

The Bear Club Grows by One

One of the happiest days up north was when my sister and I discovered that Oscoda now had a $2 movie theater in town. We discovered this while wandering around the little city center one sunny afternoon and both of us loving a cheap movie and a big bag of movie popcorn, were thrilled. In fact we decided to head into town that night and see the second-run showing of a Goldie Hawn movie; can't remember which one. What a joy to sit in a down-home movie theater, munching on popcorn and knowing we were soon to be heading back to the cabin for a good night's rest.

After the movie we got in the car and headed west on the River Road Byway, quickly leaving the lights and sounds of our favorite up north town behind. Ahead of us lay quickly enveloping forests and a long peaceful stretch of road, on which we'd be surprised to see any other cars mid week at night.

On the flat, straight and slightly sloping River Road, it is tempting to step on the gas and see what your car will do as you open up. Not advisable though as you quickly realize that the woods just to your left and right are filled with the beautiful glow of deer eyes and the tentative nocturnal explorations of raccoons and opossums.

As we turned onto Cooke Dam Road heading towards the cabin, out of habit and necessity Amanda slowed down. The night was pitch black, the forest dark. We were in the middle of a conversation when both of us saw something moving quickly on the side of the road, and heading towards our car, intending to run right in front of us. My sister slammed on her brakes just in time to let a very frightened and frantic baby black bear run in front of her car, across the road and safely into the protective arms of the forest on the other side, and most likely to mama bear too.

"Oh my gosh", we both said as one. We stopped in the middle of the road, astonished and stunned for a minute. "Wow, that was really cool", I said as we drove away. "So glad you were able to stop". We breathed a sigh of relief and smiled together at the new adventure. I mentioned to her that she was now eligible for membership into the Bear Club, at which she seemed pretty pleased.

Remembering all of our beloved dogs, past and present,
who have walked through the woods with us:

Chance
Lucky
Brindie
Bandit
Scrappy
Molly
Stanley
Lowie
Flip
Coco
Pal
Love
Belle
Jasper
Mason
Socks
Sonia
Honey
Zigy
and
Cookie

EPILOGUE

December 4, 2005 was a bright and very cold Michigan Sunday morning. I got a phone call from my mom; I could tell she'd been crying and still was. Through her tears, she relayed the family news; my Aunt Shirley had passed away an hour before.

Aunt Shirley had been fighting cancer and all the painful side-effects from chemo for the past two years. Sometimes she felt good; much of the time she was listless and in a good deal of pain.

When I spoke to my aunt about her memories of the cabin for this book, it was a struggle for her to talk to me; she stopped often for a deep breath but insisted on finishing. I worried and wondered at the time that she might not still be with us when I finally finished writing.

She lived a full year after I talked to her for her story. Her death was sorrowful to all who knew her, because everyone who knew her loved her. None of us wanted to see her in pain anymore, so we look upon her passing as a release for her.

She lived a full, happy, loving and giving life.

I am comforted in these days after her death in knowing that the last words I said to her a month before she died, were "I love you Aunt Shirley". And her last words to me were "and I love you too".